METABOLIC CONFUSION DIET

Reach Lasting Weight Loss with Revolutionary Nutrition and Fitness Strategies to Boost Metabolism and Fat Burning | With 126-Day Meal Plan

Sophie Turner

SCAN THE QR CODE

Scroll to the end to get the bonus

2 BONUS for you!

Day 25: Leg Day & HIIT
Warm-up: Leg swings, squats, and lunges – 5 min
Strength Training:
Squats: 4 sets of 10 reps
Deadlifts: 4 sets of 8 reps
Lunges: 3 sets of 12 reps per leg
HIIT Circuit:
20 seconds of mountain climbers
20 seconds of jump lunges
20 seconds rest
Repeat 5 times

Day 26: Full Body Circuit Training
Circuit (Repeat 4 times):
10 push-ups
15 V-ups

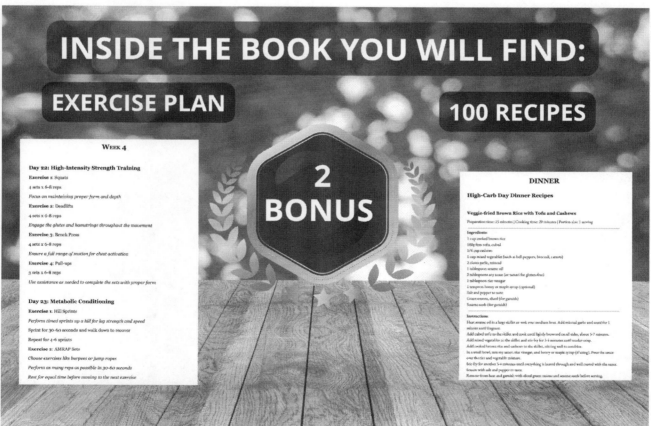

INSIDE THE BOOK YOU WILL FIND:

EXERCISE PLAN

100 RECIPES

2 BONUS

WEEK 4

Day 22: High-Intensity Strength Training
Exercise 1: Squats
4 sets x 6-8 reps
Focus on maintaining proper form and depth
Exercise 2: Deadlifts
4 sets x 6-8 reps
Engage the glutes and hamstrings throughout the movement
Exercise 3: Bench Press
4 sets x 5-8 reps
Ensure a full range of motion for chest activation
Exercise 4: Pull-ups
3 sets x 6-8 reps
Use assistance as needed to complete the sets with proper form

Day 23: Metabolic Conditioning
Exercise 1: Hill Sprints
Perform timed sprints up a hill for leg strength and speed
Sprint for 30-60 seconds and walk down to recover
Repeat for 4-6 sprints
Exercise 2: AMRAP Sets
Choose exercises like burpees or jump ropes
Perform as many reps as possible in 30-60 seconds
Rest for equal time before moving to the next exercise

DINNER

High-Carb Day Dinner Recipes

Veggie-fried Brown Rice with Tofu and Cashews
Preparation time: 15 minutes | Cooking time: 20 minutes | Portion size: 1 serving

Ingredients:
1 cup cooked brown rice
100g firm tofu, cubed
1/4 cup cashews
1 cup mixed vegetables (such as bell peppers, broccoli, carrots)
2 cloves garlic, minced
1 tablespoon sesame oil
2 tablespoons soy sauce (or tamari for gluten-free)
1 tablespoon rice vinegar
1 teaspoon honey or maple syrup (optional)
Salt and pepper to taste
Green onions, sliced (for garnish)
Sesame seeds (for garnish)

Instructions:
Heat sesame oil in a large skillet or wok over medium heat. Add minced garlic and sauté for 1 minute until fragrant.
Add cubed tofu to the skillet and cook until lightly browned on all sides, about 5-7 minutes.
Add mixed vegetables to the skillet and stir-fry for 3-4 minutes until tender-crisp.
Add cooked brown rice and cashews to the skillet, stirring well to combine.
In a small bowl, mix soy sauce, rice vinegar, and honey or maple syrup (if using). Pour the sauce over the rice and vegetable mixture.
Stir-fry for another 3-4 minutes until everything is heated through and well coated with the sauce.
Season with salt and pepper to taste.
Remove from heat and garnish with sliced green onions and sesame seeds before serving.

TABLE OF CONTENTS

PREFACE

How This Book Can Help You

Without the right support, starting a path to improve your health can seem overwhelming. With the help of this book's thorough road map and evidence-based tactics, you can achieve long-term weight loss and metabolic flexibility. Achieving long-lasting change is possible when you are armed with pertinent information and useful instruments.

The groundwork is laid in the introductory chapters, which provide concise explanations of important terms and ideas. You'll learn how metabolism controls energy balance and how it affects weight management. Common myths are dispelled as the science and historical background of metabolic confusion techniques are discussed. Now that you have this fundamental knowledge, you can proceed with facts in hand and confidence.

Expanding upon that foundation, the book explores real-world implementation. You'll discover how a healthy diet supplies the energy needed for a metabolism that operates at its best. Each macronutrient—proteins, carbohydrates, and fats—is thoroughly examined in terms of its significance. Additionally included are important micronutrients like vitamins and minerals. Guidelines for hydration speed up metabolic processes. Strategies for scheduling meals improve outcomes. Prioritizing diversity and balance positions you for sustained adherence.

With your extensive knowledge of nutrition, you will be prepared to use metabolic confusion techniques to create a personalized diet plan. Macronutrient ratios, carb cycling, and strategic calorie cycling are all well discussed. Creating a sustainable dietary plan that suits your individual needs and tastes is the goal. This offers an adaptable foundation for sustained success.

It also discusses how exercise and metabolism interact. You'll discover how developing muscle that burns calories through strength training promotes metabolic wellness. There is discussion of several cardio exercise regimens. An explanation of the metabolic advantages of high-intensity interval training is provided. To optimize outcomes, advice is given on integrated fitness programming and appropriate recuperation.

Advanced nutritional techniques build on your foundation to increase metabolic flexibility. Other methods including as carb cycling, keto diets, and intermittent fasting provide an alternative to traditional calorie restriction. Supplements for further metabolic assistance are covered. Intuitive and seasonal eating helps you become more in tune with your body's natural cycles. Finding a strategy that you can live with is the aim.

The impact of lifestyle factors on metabolism, such as gut health, stress management, and sleep, is also examined. Establishing a setting that supports your objectives puts you in a position to succeed over time. Long-lasting change is achievable when all factors influencing metabolic health are taken into consideration.

Through adaptable strategies that turn knowledge into action, you'll discover how to monitor your progress and make necessary adjustments. Solving problems averts a train wreck. This gives you all the skills you need to win the adventure and navigate it successfully.

Now that you have solutions that are supported by evidence and drawn from the most recent scientific research, you can take control of your weight management and achieve long-term metabolic health and fitness. This book will serve as your guide on the voyage that lies ahead.

Expected Outcomes

It's motivating to have a vision of the positive outcomes ahead. This foresight provides direction and incentivizes consistency when challenges arise. By highlighting the many benefits that metabolic flexibility can bring, you can stay focused on your destination.

Improved energy levels are an early win. Balanced blood sugar control prevents energy crashes and fluctuations. Efficient fuel utilization gives you steady vitality to embrace each day. You'll notice daily tasks and exercise require less effort. Enthusiasm replaces fatigue.

Accelerating fat burning kicks weight loss into high gear. Strategic metabolic confusion techniques, such as carb cycling, keep your body guessing, spurring adaptations that unlock stored fat for energy. As you build calorie-burning muscle, your metabolism receives an upgrade. The scale ticks down steadily while you increase strength and fitness.

Mental clarity improves dramatically. Stable blood sugar provides consistent energy for the brain. Hormonal balance reduces brain fog. Quality nutrition supercharges focus and concentration. You'll achieve elevated performance at work and other cognitive tasks.

Emotional balance stabilizes. Reliable energy and hormone regulation help maintain an even keel. Confidence is derived from achieving fitness goals and seeing progress. You keep stress in perspective. Each day brings poise, optimism, and good spirits.

Chronic disease risk plummets. Obesity, heart disease, diabetes, and other conditions are driven by metabolic dysfunction. As you increase flexibility and optimize wellness, risk profiles improve across the board. You extend your health and longevity.

Cardiovascular function strengthens. Exercise and balanced nutrition reduce inflammatory factors that impede circulation. Efficient fat metabolism clears triglycerides from the blood vessels. Oxygen and nutrients flow smoothly, boosting endurance. Heart health reaches new heights.

Digestion improves dramatically. A fiber-rich diet, probiotic foods, and hydration keep digestion regular and comfortable. Bloating and discomfort fade. Nutrient absorption increases to properly fuel your body. Elimination becomes effortless.

Hunger and cravings normalize. Balanced blood sugar and hormones help regulate signals of hunger and satisfaction. Quality whole foods provide steady nourishment. Mindful eating reconnects you with your body's needs.

You gain the ability to maintain your health throughout your life. The knowledge and habits you implement become second nature. You can adapt flexibly as life evolves. Each positive outcome circulates back to motivate continued progress.

This journey requires commitment and perseverance, but the rewards are life-changing. You will uncover levels of health, energy, and wellbeing you may have never considered possible. Your best self awaits, equipped with the wisdom of metabolic flexibility. Let this vision guide you on each step forward.

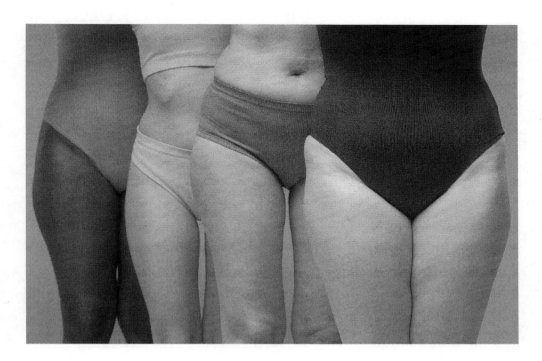

The Basics of Metabolism

All the chemical processes that sustain life comprise metabolism. These processes convert food into energy and produce the building blocks of proteins, lipids, nucleic acids, and carbohydrates that are vital for our cells and tissues. Understanding how our metabolism works provides key insights into optimizing health and facilitating weight loss.

At its most fundamental level, metabolism involves anabolism and catabolism. Anabolism consists of metabolic processes that construct molecules from smaller units, requiring an input of energy. Catabolism breaks down organic matter, releasing energy.

The macronutrients we consume—carbohydrates, fats, and proteins—are metabolized in different ways. The body breaks down carbohydrates into glucose, which circulates in the bloodstream and provides energy for cells. The liver and muscles can store excess glucose as glycogen. Between meals, one can draw upon the accessible energy reserve of glycogen.

The body breaks down dietary fats and lipids into fatty acids and glycerol. The citric acid cycle and beta-oxidation can use fatty acids for energy production. They are also important structural components of cell membranes. Glycerol feeds into glycolysis, a process that generates ATP.

Hydrolysis of proteins produces amino acids, which can act as precursors for glucose or ketones. We also use amino acids to construct new proteins and other biologically significant molecules.

The **basal metabolic rate** (BMR) is the minimum energy requirement to sustain vital bodily functions at rest. It is influenced by factors like organ mass, fat-free mass, age, and sex. People with more muscle mass tend to have higher BMRs.

Components that contribute to BMR include:

- Liver metabolism: The liver performs many essential tasks, like processing nutrients and toxins. This expends a significant amount of energy.

- Brain metabolism: The brain is a major consumer of energy, using 20% of that energy at rest. Neurons require ample glucose to meet metabolic demands.

- Heart work: The heart constantly pumps blood, necessitating high energy requirements. Cardiac muscle metabolism relies heavily on fat oxidation.

- Kidney function: Filtration and reabsorption of nutrients and wastes in the kidneys demand consistent energy input.

- Skeletal muscle: While at rest, muscles maintain tension and cellular processes requiring ATP turnover.

The **thermic effect of food** (TEF) refers to the energy expended through digesting, absorbing, and metabolizing food and nutrients. This constitutes around 10% of total energy expenditure. Macronutrients require varying levels of energy to metabolize.

Factors influencing TEF include:

- Macronutrient composition: protein elicits the greatest TEF, requiring 20–35% of the calories consumed for metabolizing. Carbohydrates require 5–15%, while fat requires 0-3%.

- Food intake: Consuming larger meals makes digestion more metabolically expensive.

- Meal frequency: More frequent meals spur a higher TEF.

- Gut microbiota: The composition of the gut microbiome impacts how efficiently food is extracted.

Physical activity is the final component of energy expenditure. This can vary substantially between individuals depending on exercise habits and lifestyle factors. Activities like fidgeting, walking, or household chores increase calorie burn above the BMR and TEF levels. Purposeful exercise like cardio or strength training expends even more energy.

In order to lose weight, energy expenditure must exceed caloric intake over time. Creating this deficit requires an appreciation of how metabolism functions. Tracking metrics like BMR and designing eating and exercise regimens to match goals allows for targeted fat loss.

What is Metabolic Confusion?

Metabolic confusion refers to the deliberate manipulation of diet, exercise, and lifestyle habits in order to prevent the body's metabolism from adapting to changes. This forces the body to continuously adjust, enhancing fat burning and making weight loss more achievable.

The idea behind metabolic confusion is that the body prefers homeostasis and will adapt to any routine. When the body becomes accustomed to certain calorie levels or workout regimens, it learns how to conserve energy and match intake with expenditure. This plateau can stall weight-loss efforts.

Metabolic confusion techniques aim to keep the body guessing, spurring it to burn extra calories. Strategically varying nutrition and training prompt physiological adaptation that boosts metabolism.

Here are some **key methods** used to create metabolic confusion:

- Calorie cycling: altering caloric intake regularly, such as by consuming higher and lower amounts in a structured pattern. This contrasts periods of calorie surplus and deficit.

- Macronutrient manipulation: varying the ratio of protein, fats, and carbohydrates rather than keeping them static. Ketogenic dieting and carb cycling exemplify this technique.

- Exercise variation: changing the type, intensity, duration, and frequency of workouts frequently while incorporating adequate rest phases. This includes diverse modalities like strength training, HIIT, and cardio.

- Meal timing: strategically shifting when meals are consumed, such as with intermittent fasting approaches. Eating earlier, later, or allowing for periods without food intake creates change.

- Food choices: substituting food items regularly so that the body doesn't adapt to any specific meal plan. Emphasizing nutrient-dense, minimally processed options.

Several **physiological mechanisms** contribute to metabolic confusion's effectiveness:

- Enhanced mitochondrial efficiency: The mitochondria must work harder to adapt to calorie spikes and deficits. This builds their capacity to metabolize energy.

- Prevention of adaptive thermogenesis: Varying caloric intake hinders the drop in resting metabolic rate that often accompanies steady dieting.

- Increased catecholamine release: frequent dietary changes stimulate greater catecholamine secretion, driving lipolysis.

- Improved insulin sensitivity: Preventing prolonged exposure to high carbohydrate intake enhances insulin receptor functioning and stability.

- Mitigation of fatigue: Changing workouts frequently reduces overuse and strains different muscle groups, lessening fatigue.

- Greater calorie burn: Both the thermic effect of food and excess post-exercise oxygen consumption (EPOC) increase, amplifying energy expenditure.

To implement a metabolic confusion style **plan**:

- Gradually transition: Allow the body to adjust to change in a stepwise manner to avoid extreme shocks.

- Plan ahead: Designate specific periods for manipulating calories, carbs, workouts, and more. The schedule changes consistently.

- Incorporate variety: include diverse foods and training modes; don't repeatedly alternate between only a couple.

- Monitor progress: Track results like weight, measurements, body fat percentage, and metabolic markers.

- Adjust as needed: Increase manipulation frequency if fat loss plateaus. Provide periods of metabolic rest when necessary.

- Prevent underfueling: Low calories and carbs are a tactic, not a permanent approach. Ensure adequate overall intake.

- Strength training: Weightlifting provides needed stimulus; match protein intake to support muscle.

Metabolic confusion necessitates strategic eating and training tailored to each individual. When executed appropriately, it jolts the metabolism to spur renewed fat burning. Sustaining progress depends on applying structured variety.

Historical Development of Metabolic Confusion

While metabolic confusion has garnered significant attention recently, the concept of varying nutrition and training to spur fat loss has been around for decades. Understanding the origins and evolution of metabolic confusion sheds light on the emergence and refinement of these techniques over time.

Early Roots

The essential notion of confusing the metabolism dates back to the 1950s and 1960s. During this time, some in the bodybuilding community began experimenting with varying caloric intake to push past plateaus. The most common approach was carb cycling, where high- and low-carb days were alternated.

The late 1960s saw the rise of more extreme "crash" diets consisting of very low calories and carbs for short periods of time. While these aggressive tactics delivered rapid results, they often proved too difficult to maintain long-term. Still, the dramatic fat loss demonstrated the power of shocking the metabolism.

Popularization in the 1980s and 1990s

In the 1980s, researchers took greater interest in how varying dietary components influenced weight loss and body composition. Studies confirmed that fluctuating caloric intake could help mitigate metabolic adaptation during dieting. Exercise scientists also began investigating the benefits of periodization in strength training.

The concept of cardio-interval training took hold during this period as well. Alternating between higher and lower intensity exercise became a core tenet of strategies to increase calorie burn and boost metabolism.

This collective research validated that reducing metabolic confusion through nutrition and training could offer measurable benefits. The term itself began circulating to describe these cutting-edge fat-loss techniques.

Key proponents like Dan Duchaine and Dr. Mauro Di Pasquale expanded on the metabolic confusion ideology and popularized its principles. Their books and courses instructed readers on how to cycle between higher-calorie and lower-calorie carb periods to optimize fat burning. These teachings reached a wide audience and fueled further interest.

Refinement and individualization

The 1990s and 2000s saw more precise and tailored approaches to metabolic confusion. New diet styles, like the anabolic diet, integrate structured high-fat and high-carb phases. Researchers continued documenting the particular physiological adaptations triggered by nutritional manipulation.

Exercise programming also evolved to incorporate undulating periodization and greater customization based on individual recovery needs and abilities. Technologies like heart rate monitoring enable more targeted cardio training.

The internet's rise facilitated the sharing of personalized metabolic confusion templates. Mobile apps have made tracking calorie and macronutrient intake easier than ever.

Current best practices

Today, technology and research support more individualized implementation of metabolic confusion techniques.

- Metabolic testing assesses baseline rates and fat-burning capability.

- Activity trackers document energy expenditure from workouts and daily movement.

- Apps structure meal plans and generate grocery lists to simplify nutrition.

- DNA analysis and blood testing identify unique genotype differences that influence responses.

- Online calculators estimate calorie and macro needs based on parameters like body composition, activity levels, and goals.

- Social media provides camaraderie, advice, and accountability in executing plans.

- Scientific understanding of optimal protein intake, nutrient timing, and ideal rest periods allows programming customization.

Though it originated in bodybuilding circles, metabolic confusion has gained mainstream acceptance due to its efficacy when applied properly. Continual assessment and evolution of techniques sustain success.

Scientific Foundations of Metabolic Flexibility

Metabolic flexibility refers to the ability to readily adapt to utilizing different fuels based on availability, such as carbs, fats, and proteins. Those with higher metabolic flexibility can more efficiently switch between burning glycogen, fatty acids, and ketones. Enhancing this flexibility allows the body to become a highly responsive fat-burning machine.

The science underlying metabolic flexibility offers crucial insights into its optimization:

Substrate Switching

Metabolic flexibility relies on substrate switching between oxidative and glycolytic pathways in response to changes in nutritional state. After a meal, glucose uptake increases, and glycogen stores are replenished. During fasting, lipolysis and fatty acid oxidation rise to spare glucose.

Flexibility depends on modulating the activity of metabolic pathways and the expression of rate-limiting enzymes through gene regulation. For example, fasting triggers transcriptional coactivators like PGC-1α that boost fat metabolism.

Mitochondrial Health

Mitochondria are metabolic hubs that dynamically adjust their density, capacity, and efficiency based on energy demands. Greater mitochondrial content and respiratory capacity enhance metabolic flexibility.

Exercise, calorie restriction, and environmental stressors stimulate mitochondrial biogenesis. This expands overall mitochondrial mass and function. Maintaining a robust mitochondrial network is key.

Insulin Sensitivity

Insulin resistance impairs metabolic switching between the fed and fasted states. Blunted postprandial insulin signaling reduces glucose uptake. Elevated basal insulin inhibits lipolysis.

Strategies like exercise, calorie restriction, and reducing inflammatory triggers improve insulin sensitivity. This restores proper metabolic responses to fed and fasted cues.

Adipose Tissue Function

Fat cells must effectively store and release lipids in response to insulin, catecholamines, and other regulators. Dysfunctional adipose tissue disturbs this balance through excessive or insufficient lipolysis.

Smaller adipocytes have more metabolic flexibility. Enhancing adipocyte insulin sensitivity, mitochondrial function, and lipolytic machinery optimizes flexibility.

Appetite Regulation

To adaptively regulate appetite, key hypothalamic circuits integrate signals about nutritional status and energy availability. Dysregulation of these pathways leads to a mismatch between hunger, caloric intake, and expenditure that reduces metabolic flexibility.

Meal timing, macronutrient manipulation, and fasting are strategies that use appetite regulation to align eating patterns with metabolic fuel shifting capacity.

Muscle Metabolism

Muscles exhibit plasticity when utilizing intramuscular glycogen, triglycerides, and delivered fatty acids for energy based on diet and activity. This flexibility is maximized by preserving muscle mitochondrial content and insulin sensitivity.

The integrated nature of metabolic flexibility across tissues and biological systems necessitates a multi-faceted approach. Lifestyle strategies that target improved insulin sensitivity, mitochondrial function, substrate switching capacity, and appetite regulation combine to create lasting flexibility.

Debunking Myths About Metabolism

Misunderstandings of metabolism often lead to common myths and misconceptions. Debunking these myths provides clarity on how metabolism really works and influences weight management.

Myth: Boosting metabolism requires intense exercise.

Reality: Exercise temporarily increases metabolism through excess post-exercise oxygen consumption (EPOC), but this accounts for a small portion of daily calorie burn. Lower-intensity activities like taking the stairs, fidgeting, or doing chores make substantial cumulative differences. Building muscle via resistance training increases the resting metabolic rate (RMR) more than intense cardio.

Myth: A faster metabolism is always better.

Reality: An overly elevated metabolism can lead to muscle wasting, immunosuppression, oxidative stress, and inadequate nutrient absorption. A responsive metabolism that can shift between fed and fasted states is ideal. Sustainably enhancing metabolism requires a balanced approach.

Myth: Metabolism steadily declines with age.

Reality: While RMR does gradually decrease by 1-2% per decade after age 30, this varies significantly by individual. Maintaining muscle mass through strength training largely mitigates age-related metabolic slowing. Other lifestyle factors, such as sleep, stress management, and nutrition choices, outweigh the effects of aging.

Myth: Eating frequently stokes metabolism.

Reality: The thermic effect of food causes a minimal metabolic boost from eating more often. Total calorie intake matters more than meal frequency. Eating too often can backfire, leading to overconsumption and poor insulin regulation. Time-restricted feeding provides metabolic benefits.

Myth: Skipping breakfast slows metabolism.

Reality: Despite claims that skipping breakfast slows metabolism, research does not demonstrate significant differences in RMR between breakfast eaters and skippers when total calories are equal. Practicality and individual variances determine ideal meal timing.

Myth: Slow metabolism thwarts weight loss.

Reality: Resting metabolism varies within 200–300 calories between people of the same age, weight, and sex. A "slow" metabolism cannot singlehandedly prevent weight loss given an appropriate caloric deficit. Creating this deficit sustainably is what matters most.

Myth: Certain foods or supplements supercharge metabolism.

Reality: No specific food or supplement inherently speeds up metabolism. Thermogenic compounds like capsaicin provide a negligible, temporary increase. Whole foods that provide nutrients, fiber, and protein support metabolism in the context of an overall healthy diet.

Myth: Yo-yo dieting ruins your metabolism forever.

Reality: Weight cycling does not permanently damage the metabolism. Adaptive thermogenesis during weight loss causes a temporary metabolic slowdown that reverses after returning to the initial weight. Sustainable lifestyle changes enable long-term metabolic improvements.

Myth: You cannot manipulate your metabolism.

Reality: Metabolic flexibility responds well to targeted nutritional interventions like calorie cycling, carb cycling, fasting regimens, and meal timing. Cardio and strength training also improve metabolism. Genetics sets the baseline, not the limits.

Debunking common metabolism myths empowers a better understanding of realistic expectations. Small daily choices related to sleep, nutrition, and training cumulatively make the biggest difference in metabolic health over the long run.

Chapter 2: Foundations of Nutrition for Metabolic Confusion

Macronutrients and Their Roles

When it comes to nutrition for metabolic health, macronutrients form the foundation of any diet. Macronutrients are nutrients that provide calories or energy; these include carbohydrates, proteins, and fats. Understanding the unique roles that each macronutrient plays is essential for structuring an eating plan that supports metabolic flexibility.

Carbohydrates are the body's preferred source of energy. During digestion, carbohydrates are broken down into glucose, which enters the bloodstream. The body then uses this glucose to fuel its cells. Carbs are especially important for fueling the brain and working muscles during physical activity.

Not all carbs are created equal. Simple carbohydrates possess a fundamental chemical structure and undergo rapid digestion. This leads to spikes in blood sugar and insulin. Examples include sugars like sucrose and high-fructose corn syrup. Complex carbohydrates have a more complicated chemical structure and take longer to break down. This provides a steady release of glucose over time. Examples include whole grains, legumes, fruits, and starchy vegetables.

For metabolic health, the focus should be on consuming more complex, nutrient-dense carbs. These provide sustained energy and contain fiber, vitamins, and minerals. Meanwhile, intake of refined and processed carbs should be limited.

You can adjust the total carb intake to meet your individual needs and goals. For instance, very low-carb or ketogenic diets restrict carbs to promote fat burning. Moderate carb diets, where around 40–50% of calories come from carbs, are common for active individuals. High-carb diets with 60% or more calories from carbs may benefit endurance athletes.

Other factors, such as carb quality, meal frequency, and timing, can also impact metabolic response beyond daily carb intake. This is where carb cycling and strategic intake in conjunction with workouts come into play.

Proteins are vital for building, repairing, and maintaining muscle tissue. Without adequate protein intake, the body will break down muscle for fuel, which slows metabolism. Protein also regulates hunger signals, blood sugar control, and other metabolic functions.

During digestion, proteins are broken down into amino acids; these amino acids act as the building blocks for new proteins. Amino acids are also involved in making hormones, enzymes, and neurotransmitters that influence metabolism.

Animal foods like meat, eggs, and dairy provide complete proteins with all the essential amino acids. Plant-based proteins like beans, nuts, grains, and soy contain varying amounts of essential aminos. Vegans may need a variety of plant proteins to get all the essential amino acids.

The RDA for protein is 0.8 grams per kilogram of bodyweight, or 0.36 grams per pound. Active individuals need more—generally 1.2 to 2 grams per kilogram or 0.5 to 1 gram per pound. A higher protein intake preserves muscle during fat loss.

Spreading protein intake evenly throughout the day provides a steady supply of amino acids for lean mass retention and metabolic support.

Dietary fats provide energy, support vitamin absorption, and play numerous other roles related to hormones, cell membranes, and tissue health. Fat provides 9 calories per gram—more than double the 4 calories per gram from carbs and protein.

There are different types of fats: saturated, monounsaturated, and polyunsaturated fats. Focusing on unsaturated plant-based fats such as avocados, nuts, seeds, and olive oil optimizes metabolic health, according to research.

Saturated fats from animal foods and trans fats found in processed items may negatively impact metabolic markers when consumed in excess. However, some saturated fat is necessary, and healthy fats should not be severely restricted.

High-fat, very-low-carb ketogenic diets rely on fat as the main energy source and have shown benefits for metabolic health. But for most people, 20–35% of calories from fat are recommended for balance.

Strategic nutrition that optimizes macronutrient intake allows you to achieve a peak metabolic state that burns fat while maintaining lean muscle mass. You need to customize your eating plan to meet your specific needs and goals.

Micronutrients: Vitamins and Minerals

While macronutrients provide the calories and energy for metabolism, micronutrients play key roles in regulating metabolic processes. Micronutrients are essential vitamins and minerals that enable the body to perform vital metabolic chemical reactions. Even minor deficiencies in certain micronutrients can hamper metabolic function and health.

Vitamins act as coenzymes throughout the body. They help convert macronutrients into energy and assist with building cellular structures and chemicals that impact metabolic pathways. The B-complex vitamins like B6, B12, and folate play particularly important roles in energy metabolism. Vitamin D also has an impact on metabolic processes. Antioxidant vitamins like C, E, and A neutralize free radicals that can damage cells and impact metabolism.

With fat-soluble vitamins like A, D, E, and K, excess intake can lead to toxicity. However, water-soluble B vitamins and vitamin C are generally safe at high supplemental doses. Consuming a variety of vitamin-rich whole foods ensures adequate intake of all vitamins without the risk of megadosing isolated forms.

Minerals serve structural, regulatory, and functional roles for optimal health and metabolism. For instance, calcium supports bone metabolism, iodine regulates thyroid hormones, iron carries oxygen in the blood, and sodium balances fluids. Many minerals act as electrolytes that manage hydration, blood pressure, and muscle function.

The main minerals involved in metabolism are chromium, calcium, iron, iodine, magnesium, potassium, selenium, sodium, and zinc. Deficiencies in any of these can hinder metabolic processes. Getting enough minerals from whole foods or targeted supplementation helps prevent metabolic disruptions.

- Calcium helps regulate fat metabolism and supports weight management when consumed through dairy products as part of a balanced diet. Studies suggest calcium supplements alone don't provide the same metabolic benefits.
- Chromium enhances the effects of insulin so the body can properly metabolize carbohydrates, fats, and proteins. Altering chromium levels may benefit those with metabolic disorders like diabetes.
- Iodine is required for normal thyroid hormone production, which regulates metabolism. Low iodine levels can cause hypothyroidism, fatigue, and weight gain.
- Iron carries oxygen in the blood to all tissues, including muscles. Low iron levels reduce oxygen delivery during exercise and hinder performance. Iron levels can drop on calorie-restricted diets.
- Magnesium supports over 300 metabolic reactions involving glucose, fat, and protein. Magnesium also moderates stress hormones that can impact metabolism. Many Americans don't get enough magnesium.
- Potassium helps regulate fluid balance, cardiovascular function, and nerve signals. It also reduces sodium's effects on blood pressure. Deficiencies are rare, but they can occur with prolonged vomiting, diarrhea, or certain medications.
- Selenium boosts metabolic rate, impacts thyroid hormones, and regulates antioxidant levels. A slower metabolism and difficulty losing weight may be associated with low selenium.
- Zinc is vital for metabolic enzymes, immune function, and protein synthesis. Zinc deficiencies can negatively affect leptin and insulin, slowing metabolism.

Evaluating the intake of these key vitamins and minerals can reveal potential metabolic weaknesses. Targeted supplementation alongside food sources can help correct deficiencies hindering metabolism. But megadoses should be avoided due to their possible toxicity.

With strategic nutrition and lifestyle choices, it's possible to obtain all the necessary vitamins and minerals for optimal metabolic function, leading to better health.

The Importance of Hydration

Staying properly hydrated is a key factor in maintaining a healthy metabolism and body function. Water makes up 50–70% of body weight and is essential for nearly every metabolic process. Even mild dehydration, or just 1-2% water loss, can lead to impaired cognitive and physical performance. Severe dehydration can be life-threatening.

Water regulates body temperature, lubricates joints, protects organs and tissues, and transports nutrients. It's the medium for biochemical reactions, allowing nutrients to interact and create energy. Adequate hydration enables efficient digestion, absorption, circulation, and excretion.

Water is the body's main antioxidant, counteracting damaging free radicals and inflammation. Chronic low-grade dehydration creates excess oxidative stress that can accelerate aging and disease. Optimal hydration reduces inflammation for improved metabolic and cardiovascular health.

Hydration is critical for metabolism because it allows the kidneys and liver to process toxins and waste. Water also prevents constipation and bloating, ensuring smooth metabolic function. Even mild dehydration can hinder fat breakdown and cause water retention.

Drinking sufficient water every day boosts metabolism by increasing thermogenesis—the energy spent digesting food and absorbing nutrients. Cold water may even increase calorie burn. Staying well hydrated also reduces appetite and calorie intake.

When cutting calories for fat loss, hydration becomes even more important. Dehydration, coupled with restricted eating, can stall weight loss. Drinking water helps prevent false hunger when the body is actually just thirsty. For those exercising to boost metabolism, proper hydration also optimizes performance capability.

The intake of total water from food and fluids is 3.7 liters for men and 2.7 liters for women. This equals roughly 16 cups for men and 12 cups for women. Fluid needs are higher for active people in hot climates.

Pure water is the ideal hydration source. Soda, fruit juice, coffee, and alcohol are diuretics that cause increased water loss. Energy drinks are high in caffeine and sugar. Excessive intake may lead to anxiety, insomnia, gastrointestinal distress, and metabolic disruption.

Signs of inadequate hydration include thirst, headaches, fatigue, dizziness, a dry mouth, constipation, dark urine, and muscle cramps. Checking urine color is an easy way to gauge status; light yellow indicates proper hydration, while dark yellow signifies dehydration.

Tips for staying hydrated include carrying a refillable water bottle, choosing water instead of other beverages, and tracking daily intake. Adding lemon, mint, cucumber, or fruit can boost flavor. Sparkling water provides an alternative to still water.

Electrolyte drinks, such as coconut water and low-sugar sports beverages, replenish minerals lost in sweat. Broths provide hydration along with vitamins and protein. Herbal teas and diluted fruit juices also contribute to fluid intake.

Easing into increased water consumption prevents discomfort. Spreading intake evenly throughout the day enables steady absorption and uptake. Measuring input versus output can reveal specific individual needs.

With age, the thirst mechanism weakens. Older adults are more susceptible to dehydration. Preventative hydration is key, along with monitoring urine color, fluid intake, and body weight.

In some cases, excessive water intake can dangerously dilute blood sodium levels. This is rare in healthy adults who drink normal amounts throughout the day. Those with certain conditions, like heart failure, kidney disease, or SIADH, may need personalized hydration advice.

Maintaining optimal hydration provides numerous metabolic and performance benefits. Drinking adequate water should be a simple health habit for anyone looking to boost metabolism, energy, cognition, exercise recovery, and overall well-being.

Timing Your Meals for Optimal Results

When it comes to boosting metabolism, the timing of meals and snacks can be just as important as what you eat. Aligning your intake with your body's natural circadian rhythms and activity patterns enhances digestive health while optimizing energy levels. Research shows meal timing significantly influences metabolism, body composition, and other health markers.

- The human body follows an innate 24-hour cycle known as the circadian rhythm. Hormones, body temperature, hunger levels, and other functions fluctuate throughout the day. Timing food intake to work with your body's rhythms provides metabolic advantages compared to erratic eating habits.
- In the morning, metabolism ramps up, insulin sensitivity increases, and appetite-regulating hormones like leptin and ghrelin regulate hunger signals. Eating an energizing breakfast helps the body refuel after the overnight fast. Those who skip breakfast tend to overeat later while missing out on key nutrients.
- Aim for a breakfast containing 20–35% of your daily calorie target, with a balance of complex carbs, fiber, protein, and healthy fats. Options such as an omelet with oats and fruit or Greek yogurt with nuts and berries boost AM metabolism.
- The hours immediately before and after workouts are prime times for fueling. An easily digestible pre-workout snack 30–60 minutes beforehand, such as a banana or whey protein shake, prevents low energy during exercise.
- After training, quickly consuming protein and carbs helps restock glycogen stores, stimulate muscle protein synthesis, and limit cortisol for faster recovery. Aim to eat a post-workout meal within 45 minutes.
- Energy demands and insulin sensitivity decrease as the day goes on. Saving the majority of carbohydrate intake for the first half of the day while tapering intake at night can improve body composition.
- Dinner should be the lightest meal, with a focus on lean protein, veggies, and healthy fats. Eating a big meal late promotes fat storage. Limiting carbs in the evening helps control hunger and blood sugar overnight for restful sleep.
- Beyond aligning larger meals with your body's daily rhythms, snack timing in between can provide a metabolism boost. Having a snack every 3–4 hours helps regulate blood glucose and insulin to favor fat burning over fat storage.
- Portable snacks like Greek yogurt, veggies and hummus, fresh fruit, or mixed nuts tide you over between meals while fueling your body consistently throughout the day.
- Nighttime fasting for 12–16 hours between an early dinner and the next day's breakfast allows the digestive system to rest. Avoiding late snacking enhances metabolic efficiency. To get better sleep, stop eating three hours before bed.
- However, total fasting for extended periods of time is counterproductive. Severely restricting calories, skipping meals, and prolonged fasting lead to muscle loss and a slower metabolism. Stick to time-restricted nightly fasting instead for the best results.
- While meal timing alignment with circadian rhythms offers benefits, be flexible based on commitments. The total number of calories and macronutrients over the course of each 24-hour period is also key.
- To accommodate changes in routine, adjust your eating schedule as needed. Consistency day-to-day is not required. Simply focus on eating lighter earlier, fueling up during workouts, and avoiding late snacking.

With mindful meal timing guided by your body's natural metabolic patterns, it's possible to boost fat burning, energy levels, and overall health.

Integrating Variety into Your Diet

While nutrition fundamentals, such as calories in versus calories out, ultimately dictate weight loss, eating a wide variety of healthy foods provides immense metabolic benefits. Changing your food choices naturally improves micronutrient intake while also making your diet more exciting and sustainable.

Each food offers a unique micronutrient and phytochemical profile. Eating a diverse mix maximizes your exposure to compounds that stimulate metabolism, curb inflammation, and provide satiety. A lack of variety can lead to vitamin or mineral deficiencies that derail fat loss.

For example, vibrant, deeply colored produce like sweet potatoes, berries, spinach, and tomatoes provides different antioxidants and anti-inflammatory compounds. Nuts and seeds offer an array of minerals, like magnesium, selenium, and zinc. Herbs and spices contain protective plant chemicals.

No single food item can offer complete nutrition. While supplements help fill gaps, real whole foods provide optimal nutrient absorption and synergy between compounds.

A simple way to assess variety is to check that all color groups are represented each day: red, orange, yellow, green, blue/purple, and white. A rainbow on your plate ensures a broad spectrum of phytonutrients.

In addition to produce, vary your proteins, carbs, fats, and flavor profiles. For amino acid diversity, mix together meat, dairy, eggs, plant proteins such as lentils and tofu, and seafood. Rotate through different healthy starchy carbs, whole grains, nuts, seeds, and oils.

Trying global recipes exposes you to new spices, ingredients, and compounds. Thai, Indian, Mediterranean, and Mexican cuisines offer flavorful ways to explore new foods.

Look for seasonal produce at farmer's markets and join a CSA. Sign up for a meal delivery kit offering creative recipes with uncommon ingredients. Allowing variety in your diet prevents boredom while boosting nutrition.

However, completely eliminating any food group long-term tends to backfire. Restrictive diets with little variety often end in overindulgence of off-limit items. Allowing flexibility and some treats in moderation is key to compliance.

Tips to make variety effortless:

- Stock up on frozen, canned, and shelf-stable produce to easily add to meals.
- Buy pre-chopped veggies and pre-cooked whole grains to save prep time.
- Roast a sheet pan of your favorite veggies at the start of the week for quick sides.
- Growth sprouts and microgreens can be used as garnishes and toppers.
- Add new spices to meals weekly until you find your favorites.
- Try one new produce item at the store weekly.

Meal-prepping components like proteins, grains, and chopped veggies streamline throwing together varied meals. With prepped ingredients and versatile recipes on hand, healthy eating doesn't have to become monotonous.

Bring variety to snack time too. Rotate through options like cottage cheese, hard-boiled eggs, fresh fruits and veggies, nuts, nut butter, yogurt, protein bars, or shakes. Avoid relying on the same one or two items.

While structured diet plans with set meals aid some, long-term success is more likely when you develop go-to recipes that incorporate flexibility. Allowing yourself total restriction on any food sets you up for failure.

Continue tasting new ingredients, cuisines, and seasonings; your palate and metabolism will thank you. With a commitment to trying new foods consistently, eating for fat loss and wellness becomes more pleasurable.

Introduction to Diet Planning

When it comes to achieving your health and fitness goals, what you eat matters just as much, if not more, than how you exercise. Your diet provides the necessary nutrients and fuel for your body to function optimally and thrive. Planning your meals and structuring your nutrition is a fundamental part of any exercise or weight loss program.

- To start, it's important to understand your basal metabolic rate (BMR). This represents the minimum number of calories your body needs to perform essential functions like breathing, blood circulation, and organ function. The higher your BMR, the more calories you burn at rest. Your BMR is influenced by factors like age, height, weight, and muscle mass. There are online calculators that can estimate your BMR based on your stats. Knowing this provides a baseline calorie goal.
- With metabolic confusion, the idea is to vary your caloric intake periodically to spur fat burning. So you'll want to calculate a calorie deficit below your BMR—typically around 500 calories—for weight loss phases. Then allow for periods of muscle building at maintenance or above. Tracking apps help tally your intake against these goals.
- Calorie cycling should align with your workout schedule. On high-intensity training days, consume more carbs to fuel performance. On rest days, scale back. The timing of meals also matters; front-load calories earlier in the day. And don't skip protein at every meal to protect your muscles. Ultimately, your food choices, portions, and schedule should sync with your activities and recovery needs throughout the week.
- Incorporating variety into your diet is also key to reducing metabolic confusion. Rotate through different healthy proteins, fruits, vegetables, grains, and fats. Try new flavors and cuisines. This keeps your metabolism adaptable and avoids boredom. Meal prep makes it

easier to plan ahead while still mixing it up. Cook in batches on weekends, so quick, balanced meals are on hand all week.

- Portion control is another essential diet planning skill. Until you can visually estimate serving sizes, use measuring cups and food scales. Be mindful of calorie-dense foods like oils, cheese, nuts, and red meat. Avoid going back for seconds. Smaller plates and bowls help control overeating. Slow down and savor each bite. Stop eating when you feel satisfied and not overly full.
- As for what to eat, focus on whole, minimally processed foods—lean proteins, produce, whole grains, legumes, healthy fats, and dairy. Limit sweets, salty snacks, sugary drinks, and refined carbs like white bread, as these provide empty calories. Moderation of treats is okay. Beware of trendy exclusion diets that ban entire food groups unless medically indicated.
- A general healthy plate model for balanced nutrition is 1/2 non-starchy vegetables, 1/4 whole grains or starches, 1/4 lean protein, plus fruit, dairy, or plant fats as desired. Tailor this template to your calorie needs and preferences. Don't obsess over perfection; just make mostly wholesome choices.
- Drinking water throughout the day helps you stay hydrated. Herbal tea and black coffee also count. Limit alcohol and sugary beverages. Make sure to get adequate fiber from fruits, vegetables, beans, nuts, and whole grains to stay regular.

While structured diet plans provide helpful guidance at the start, learning flexible, mindful eating habits is the real key to sustainable success. Keep variety, moderation, and balance in mind. Adjust your portions and food choices as needed to align with your body's signals and changing routine. Don't succumb to restrictive dieting. Nourish your body well for the long haul.

Cycling Your Calories

Calorie cycling is a strategic approach to eating that involves varying your daily calorie intake over designated periods of time. This technique can enhance fat-loss efforts while also supporting muscle growth when paired with proper exercise. Calorie cycling works by keeping your metabolism guessing, preventing adaptation when your body compensates for restricted calories.

1. First, determine your basal metabolic rate (BMR)—the minimum calories needed for basic functioning. Online calculators can estimate your BMR using inputs like age, weight, and height. This is your maintenance level for weight stability. To lose fat, you'll cycle between a calorie deficit below your BMR and higher calorie periods. A moderate daily deficit of 500 calories equates to approximately 1 pound lost per week.
2. Now decide your calorie cycling durations. Common frameworks cycle weekly or monthly. For example, 3 weeks in deficit followed by 1 week at maintenance or above. Longer cycles allow greater deficits for enhanced fat burning, while shorter cycles limit metabolic slowing. Start conservatively to assess tolerance.
3. Next, use your BMR to determine calorie amounts for deficit versus non-deficit periods. Aim for a maximum daily deficit of 500–750 calories during low periods for steady weight loss without starvation. On higher-calorie days, aim for maintenance or 10–15% above. The larger the gap between cycles, the more pronounced the metabolic stimulus.
4. During calorie deficit stints, maintain a high protein intake of around 0.7–1 gram per pound of body weight to preserve muscle. Limit processed carbs and added sugars that trigger hunger. Focus on fiber-rich complex carbs, healthy fats, and lean proteins to maximize satiety. Multivitamins help get sufficient micronutrients.
5. On higher-calorie days, increase carbs to replenish glycogen stores. The extra calories can come from wholesome complex carbs, plant fats, and proteins. You may also work on a treat

meal; just don't overdo it. Still emphasize protein on all days. When there is a calorie surplus properly timed training helps direct excess calories toward muscle growth.

6. Calorie distribution within days is also important. Frontload your calories in the morning and early afternoon. This aligns with your circadian rhythm, so excess calories are metabolized rather than stored as fat. Have a substantial breakfast with protein, complex carbs, and fruit. Also, get adequate fuel before workouts.

7. Hunger management is key to compliance. Drink plenty of water and eat high-fiber foods with healthy fats to control your appetite. Within meals, emphasize proteins and veggies first. Schedule meals regularly. Listen to internal hunger and fullness cues.

8. Avoid drastic calorie swings and deprivation, which can trigger binges or metabolic downregulation. Moderation during higher-calorie periods is still advised. Discipline and consistency over the long haul lead to the best body composition outcomes.

9. Calorie cycling calculators or tracking apps can be used to map out daily numbers aligned with your plan framework. Apps help tally calories for accuracy. You don't have to be perfect every day, just overall. Weigh yourself weekly to gauge progress, but not daily. Take measurements, as the scale may plateau during muscle-building phases.

10. Adapt plans based on results, energy levels, and sustainability. You may need to cycle at higher or lower percentages. Lengthen deficit stints if progress stalls. If you feel drained, add an extra day of high calories. Diet breaks during maintenance are fine, too.

Patience and persistence through ups and downs lead to success. Trust the calorie cycling process to reveal your fittest physique while keeping your metabolism fired up. Pair smart nutrition with consistent training for health, energy, and body confidence.

The Role of Protein in Muscle Preservation

When embarking on a fat-loss diet, it's critical to preserve lean muscle mass. Losing weight shouldn't mean losing muscle either. Adequate protein intake plays a key role in maintaining precious muscle, especially when in a calorie deficit.

To start, let's review **protein needs**. While the RDA for protein is 0.8 grams per kilogram of body weight, higher intakes are recommended for active individuals, and dieting phases target fat loss versus muscle loss. Most experts suggest 1.2-2 grams of protein per kg, equating to around 0.5–1 gram per pound. So for a 150-pound person, 75–150 grams of protein daily.

- Higher protein levels prevent muscle breakdown when calories are reduced. The body will meet energy needs by releasing amino acids via muscle protein breakdown. Consuming enough protein directly supplies amino acids, preserving muscle. Strength training also signals muscle retention; protein enables this process.
- Protein has a high thermogenic effect, requiring more calories to digest than carbs or fat. More protein increases your resting metabolic rate, supporting a calorie deficit. Protein also suppresses appetite better than less-satiating carbs or fat, allowing a lower caloric intake while feeling full.

Now let's explore **quality protein sources**. Lean meats like chicken, turkey, fish, and red meat are excellent options, providing complete essential amino acid profiles. Dairy products, including Greek yogurt, cottage cheese, and protein powders like whey and casein, also supply high-quality protein.

- Plant proteins can absolutely help with muscle building. Soy, beans, lentils, nuts, seeds, and whole grains contain decent amino acid profiles. Combine plant proteins at meals to ensure you get all the essential amino acids. Veggie burgers or plant proteins combined with rice for a complete protein meal are options.
- Protein timing is also important during workouts. Have a protein-containing meal or shake within the hour before exercise; this preps muscles for growth and recovery. Then consume protein again within 45 minutes post-workout, when muscles are primed for repair and rebuilding. Spread out protein intake at meals throughout the day, too.

Okay, now let's delve into the science of **how protein builds muscle**. When you strength train, tiny tears form in the muscle fibers. Protein provides amino acids for the repair and growth of these fibers. The hormone insulin is secreted in response to protein intake, starting the muscle-building process.

- Specific amino acids, like leucine, directly stimulate muscle protein synthesis. Leucine is the highest in animal proteins. Consuming at least 2–3 grams of leucine per meal optimizes muscle growth. Other amino acids aid recovery too. Proline and glycine supply the collagen needed for connective tissue repair.
- Your body incorporates new muscle protein into enlarged fibers through resistance training and ample protein intake, resulting in increased size and strength over time. This muscle protein synthesis process can last up to 48 hours after a workout. Protein consumed before bed may help with overnight rebuilding.
- Without sufficient protein intake, the body cannibalizes muscle to fuel its energy needs when in a calorie deficit. Low-protein diets lead to smaller, weaker muscles despite training. Dieters lose more lean mass than fat without adequate protein. To maintain metabolic rate, anti-aging effects, and athletic performance, protein is a priority!

In summary, protein truly is a dieter's best friend. At each meal and snack, prioritize protein, incorporating a variety of lean, complete protein sources. To achieve optimal results, time protein intake around workouts. Protein powers muscle retention and fat burning during calorie restriction on the path to a strong, lean physique. Support your training and metabolic confusion diet with ample, high-quality protein.

Carbohydrate Manipulation Techniques

Carbohydrates provide the body with its primary fuel source in the form of glucose. Managing carb intake is central to metabolic health and body composition goals. Techniques like carbohydrate cycling can optimize fat burning while fueling training.

Carbs get a bad rap, but grams themselves don't make you fat. Excess calories do. Carbs still influence fat storage because of their effects on insulin. This key hormone moves glucose from the blood into cells for energy. The process of lipogenesis stores excess glucose as glycogen or converts it to fat.

Lower-carb diets enhance fat loss by keeping insulin low. Through ketogenesis, the body mobilizes stored fat for fuel. However, very low carbs may negatively impact high-intensity training capacity. Strategic carb manipulation allows low-carb benefits plus workout fuel.

The simplest method is to go lower carb on rest days and higher carb around workouts. Reduce carbs to 50–100 grams on off days from exercise. On training days, increase to 2–3 grams per pound of bodyweight. Time these carbs pre-workout, during, and post-workout.

Carb cycling involves more extended low- and high-carb periods over days, weeks, or months. A basic structure is 5 days low-carb, 2 days high. Low days range from 50 to 150 grams of carbs, while high days reach up to 350 grams. High-carb days replenish muscle glycogen for the next bout of training.

The strictest form, ketogenic cycling, includes very low-carb ketogenic phases of 30–50 grams for several weeks, alternating with 1-2-day high-carb refeeds of up to 600 grams. This leverages keto's metabolic advantages while offsetting frequent training demands.

Calories still matter; even low-carb days should be at an overall deficit to drive fat loss. Protein and fat consumption stay constant, while carbs cycle up and down. Pay attention to your body's signals to find carbohydrate sweet spots for energy, performance, and metabolic adaptation.

Now let's explore how to structure filling, lower carb days for fat loss. Focus on fibrous vegetables like leafy greens, broccoli, asparagus, green beans, and peppers. They provide nutrients and bulk. Moderate servings of nuts, seeds, avocado, and oils add healthy fats.

- Pick lean proteins, including poultry, fish, and plant-based options like tofu. Enjoy full-fat dairy in moderation. Limit grains and starchy veggies. Stay very low on sugar to manage hunger and insulin. Boost electrolytes like sodium, magnesium, and potassium.
- On higher-carb days, include more fruits, starchy veggies, whole grains, and legumes. Time carb intake strategically around workouts when muscles are most insulin-sensitive and receptive to refueling. Just don't graze endlessly.
- Meal timing also optimizes carbohydrate metabolism. Consuming carbs at night leads to greater fat storage versus an equivalent morning portion. Front-load carbs in earlier meals while keeping dinner low-glycemic and lighter overall with veggies and protein.
- Listen to your body and results to fine-tune your carbohydrate intake. Moderate, well-timed carbs support training, while controlled restriction intermittently promotes fat loss via metabolic advantage—a winning combo!

With a little trial and error, carb manipulation provides the best of both worlds: enhanced fat burning from strategic low-carb days paired with well-fueled active performance. Work these techniques into your calorie cycling for maximum metabolic confusion and flexibility.

Incorporating Healthy Fats

Dietary fat has long been associated with weight gain and heart disease. However, research now shows that high-quality, unsaturated fats offer important health benefits and a place in a well-balanced diet. This chapter will look at how to incorporate healthy fat sources into your metabolic confusion plan to hit your macros, control hunger, and improve body composition.

First, let's review why **you need dietary fats** and **how much** to aim for daily. Essential fatty acids like omega-3s and omega-6s cannot be produced by the body; food is the only source. Fat aids in vitamin and mineral absorption. Fats provide the building blocks for hormones and cell membranes.

- In terms of amounts, 20–35% of total daily calories from healthy fats are recommended. On a 2000-calorie diet, that equates to 44–78 grams of fat. Too little dietary fat negatively impacts hormones, energy levels, and the absorption of fat-soluble nutrients.

Now let's explore **quality** fat sources to focus on. Unsaturated fats, including monounsaturated and polyunsaturated varieties, are anti-inflammatory and heart-healthy. Good plant sources include avocado, nuts, seeds, olive oil, and coconut oil.

- Among animal sources, fatty fish like salmon and sardines provide the anti-inflammatory omega-3 fats EPA and DHA. Grass-fed meats and pasture-raised eggs also offer beneficial fats. Saturated fats from red meat and full-fat dairy should be limited to 10% of total calories or less.
- In the kitchen, use oils like olive, avocado, and coconut for cooking, dressings, and marinades. Snack on a quarter cup of nuts or seeds. Add nut butters to smoothies. Top salads and veggies with a half sliced avocado. Grill up salmon fillets. Bake chicken thighs with the skin on.
- Prepare dressings and dips with Greek yogurt, lemon juice, and herbs. In moderation, enjoy full-fat dairy products like cheese and plain whole milk yogurt. Cook eggs in olive oil instead of butter. Add half an avocado to your breakfast.
- These whole food sources provide a balance of satiating fats plus protective compounds like antioxidants, polyphenols, and fiber. Limit processed forms like packaged snacks to minimize added sugars, salt, and refined oils.

Now let's review **how fats help you** get shredded and lean. Dietary fat enhances satiety and appetite control for fewer overall calories. Compared to carbohydrates and protein, fats slow down digestion, which helps you feel fuller for longer. Leaving you satisfied with fewer daily calories sets the stage for fat loss.

- Fats support hormones related to body composition, including testosterone, insulin, and leptin. Testosterone aids muscle building and metabolism. Insulin sensitivity ensures carbs are shuttled to muscles, not fat. Leptin regulates hunger and fat burn.
- Fats don't spike insulin like carbs, making them unlikely to convert to body fat. But calories still matter; stick to reasonable portions of even healthy fats to avoid excess intake. For optimal energy utilization, time fat consumption around physical activity.
- For best results, balance all three macros. Very low-fat or carb extremes tend to backfire long-term for sustainable fat loss. Listen to your body and fine-tune fat intake levels that provide satiation while supporting your goals.

In conclusion, incorporate healthy fats into your metabolic confusion plan. They satisfy hunger, provide essential nutrients, balance hormones, and promote lasting leanness.

CHAPTER 4: ESSENTIAL FITNESS STRATEGIES

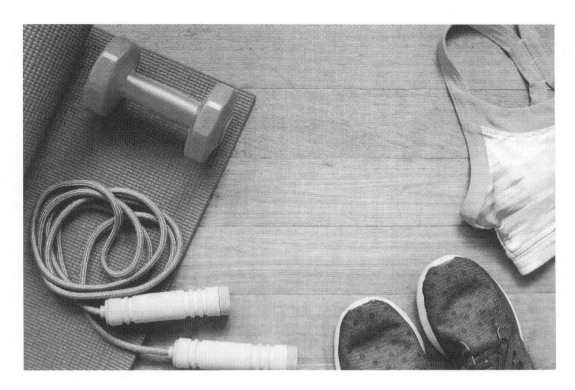

Understanding the Link Between Exercise and Metabolism

There is a close association between exercise and metabolism that affects both weight loss and general health. Physical activity causes our bodies to undergo chemical changes that promote muscular growth and fat burning. Knowing how exercise increases metabolism will help you get the most out of your routines and achieve better outcomes.

- Aerobic activity, also referred to as cardio, is any major muscle movement performed rhythmically that causes a prolonged increase in heart rate. Cardio exercises can take many forms, such as walking, running, cycling, swimming, dancing, etc. Because cardio activity requires energy to move your body, it burns fat and calories. You will require more fuel the longer and harder you practice cardio. To supply this energy need, your body uses protein, lipids, and carbohydrates that have been stored.

- Lean muscle mass is increased through weight training, sometimes referred to as resistance exercise or strength training. Because of its metabolic activity, this muscle tissue burns calories continuously. Your resting metabolism will be higher if you are more muscular. This is so because muscle helps your body achieve its basal metabolic rate, which is the bare minimum of calories required for essential life-sustaining processes. Energy is also needed for strength training exercises. Your body must supply energy to carry out the movements when you strain your muscles.

- A type of cardiovascular exercise called high-intensity interval training (HIIT) mixes brief bursts of vigorous activity with rest intervals. HIIT workouts can be performed with sprinting, cycling, jump rope, and other exercises. Through an increase in EPOC, or excess post-exercise oxygen consumption, the intensive intervals dramatically accelerate metabolism. After the workout, your body continues to burn more calories as a result of this impact, which restores equilibrium to your systems. HIIT can burn 25–30% more calories than other types of exercise, according to research.

- Exercise burns calories, but it also causes chemical processes in the body that raise your metabolic rate. Your body releases hormones like norepinephrine and adrenaline when you exercise. These hormones act as messengers, directing stored fat into cells where it is consumed for energy. After a workout, the effects may linger for several hours.

- Additionally, exercise makes you more sensitive to insulin. The hormone known as insulin is responsible for enabling the body's cells to take up and use glucose from the blood. Your cells can absorb glucose for energy or storage more effectively as your insulin sensitivity increases. Increased insulin sensitivity reduces the amount of insulin your pancreas must generate. Improving insulin sensitivity might assist your body switch from storing fat to burning it. High insulin levels can encourage the storage of fat.

- Regular exercise can improve the diversity and well-being of your gut flora. These are the trillions of bacteria that are present in your gastrointestinal tract. Studies show that having a healthy, diverse microbiome increases metabolism and helps with weight management. Exercise promotes metabolic health by altering gut flora in a beneficial way.

- Strength training enhances your resting metabolism by directly increasing muscle mass. An extra pound of muscle consumes roughly six calories a day. Even while it might not seem like much, over time, it can add up. Gaining 10 pounds of muscle means burning an additional 60 calories a day at rest. That is more than 22,000 extra calories expended in a year without any added exertion. Your body becomes a machine that burns calories when you perform resistance training.

- Exercise has indirect impacts on body weight and composition regulation in addition to its direct effects on metabolism. Exercise causes the release of endorphins, serotonin, and other substances that improve mood. This may lessen overindulgence brought on by stress and emotional eating. Exercise also provides you with increased energy and drive to maintain other health-promoting behaviors, such as enough sleep, water, and nutrition—all of which are essential for maintaining a healthy metabolism and body weight.

In conclusion, exercise raises resting metabolic rate and boosts calorie expenditure both instantly and over time. There are metabolic advantages to all types of exercise, including high-intensity interval training, strength training, and cardio. A minimum of 30 minutes of exercise three times a week can greatly increase metabolism. For optimal calorie burn and better body composition, combine diverse workout forms that test your body in different ways. Therefore, as part of your total weight reduction or maintenance regimen, take advantage of the potent synergistic metabolic advantages of exercise.

Resistance Training for Enhanced Metabolism

Resistance training, also known as strength training or weight lifting, offers powerful metabolic benefits that can boost daily calorie burn and improve body composition. The primary way that strength training enhances metabolism is by building lean muscle mass. Skeletal muscle is metabolically active tissue that burns calories around the clock to maintain itself. The more muscle you have, the higher your resting metabolism will be. Research shows that resistance training is a highly effective way to increase muscle mass and metabolic rate.

- The mechanical stress of lifting weights and performing resistance exercises breaks down your muscles during strength training sessions. This triggers a process known as muscle protein synthesis, which rebuilds the muscles with increased strength. With consistent training and proper protein intake, your muscles will begin to grow in size and strength. Bigger muscles require more energy, even at rest, causing you to burn more calories day and night. Studies indicate that each pound of additional muscle mass burns about 6 extra calories daily.
- Strength training not only builds more muscle, but it also prevents the loss of existing muscle, which commonly occurs with aging and weight loss. Maintaining muscle mass helps stabilize your metabolism against declining as you get older. Research demonstrates that resistance exercise effectively counteracts age-related muscle loss, preventing a decline in your body composition and metabolic rate over time.
- In addition to muscle-building effects, strength training provides a metabolic boost by causing excess post-exercise oxygen consumption (EPOC). This is the increased calorie burn you experience after exercise as your body works to return to homeostasis. Resistance training results in elevated EPOC that can persist for 24–48 hours. So you continue torching calories even after leaving the gym. The more intense the workout, the greater the magnitude and duration of EPOC.
- Furthermore, lifting weights increases insulin sensitivity, which impacts glucose metabolism. Insulin is the hormone that allows cells throughout the body to take up glucose from the bloodstream for energy or glycogen storage. When your tissues become more sensitive to insulin, they absorb glucose more efficiently, necessitating less insulin release from the pancreas.
- Since insulin promotes fat storage, improved insulin action helps shift your body from fat-storing to fat-burning mode. Strength training helps reverse insulin resistance, a precursor to type 2 diabetes that is common with obesity and aging. Enhancing your body's ability to manage blood glucose levels provides metabolic benefits beyond increased calorie burning.
- Resistance training also indirectly boosts metabolism by altering body composition. Your resting metabolism rises as you increase lean muscle mass and decrease body fat percentage. Muscle burns more calories than fat, both at rest and during physical activity. So, the higher your muscle-to-fat ratio, the more calories you will expend daily through your increased metabolic engine.

To gain the most metabolic benefit from resistance training, it is important to structure your strength workouts properly and stick to the program consistently. Follow these **guidelines** for optimal results:

- Train each major muscle group at least twice per week. Legs, back, chest, shoulders, arms, and core.

- Use compound movements like squats, deadlifts, rows, and presses. These involve multiple joints and maximize muscle activation.

- Lift challenging weights around the 8–12 rep range, taking sets close to muscular failure.

- Include a mix of heavier lifting days and lighter metabolic circuits.

- Allow for full recovery between training sessions. Nutrition and rest allow muscles to build.

- Progressively increase weights, volume, and intensity over time to continually challenge muscles.

- Focus on proper form and full range of motion to maximize muscle fiber activation.

- Change up your program every 4–8 weeks to keep your body adapting optimally.

Resistance training is a highly efficient way to enhance your resting metabolic rate and daily calorie burn. Strength workouts also improve body composition by building calorie-torching lean muscle mass. Follow a well-structured, progressive strength training program alongside a moderate calorie deficit to lose fat while maintaining or even gaining strength and muscle. The metabolic benefits of resistance exercise make it a fundamental component of any weight-loss or body-transformation plan.

Cardiovascular Exercises for Fat Loss

Cardiovascular exercise, also known as aerobic exercise or cardio, is any rhythmic activity that raises your heart rate and breathing for an extended period of time. Regular cardio workouts are highly effective for burning calories and body fat. Understanding how to utilize different types of cardio can help you maximize fat loss while keeping your metabolism revving.

- Cardio provides a major calorie burn because it uses large muscle groups and requires your body to take in extra oxygen. The more intensely and longer you are able to sustain cardio exercise, the more fat and calories you will incinerate during each session. In addition, cardio builds cardiovascular fitness, which allows you to work out harder and longer before reaching fatigue.
- There are many modalities you can choose from to get your heart pumping and your energy burning. Common forms of cardio ideal for fat loss include jogging, cycling, rowing, swimming, jumping rope, stair climbing, dance aerobics, and kickboxing. Any exercise you enjoy that keeps you moving for lengthy intervals is a great fat-burning choice.
- For maximum metabolic and fat-burning effects, aim to get in 150–300 minutes of moderate-intensity cardio per week or 75–150 minutes of vigorous exercise per week. You can break this up however fits your schedule, from 30- to 60-minute sessions 4-6 days per

week to longer workouts 2-3 times per week. Just be sure to elevate your heart rate to 60–85% of your maximum for extended periods in each session.

- In addition to steady-state cardio at a sustained exertion level, you can incorporate short bouts of high-intensity interval training (HIIT) into your routine. With active recovery periods, HIIT alternates short bursts of intense cardio, such as sprints, bike surges, or heavy bag work. Just 1-2 short HIIT sessions per week lasting 10–20 minutes can significantly boost your metabolism, fat burning, and cardiovascular fitness.

To optimize your cardio workouts for fat loss, focus on achieving the following training **targets**:

- Sustain an elevated heart rate continuously for 20+ minutes (at least 30–60 is ideal).

- Reach a 60-85% max heart rate based on your age and fitness level.

- Work up a sweat and feel short of breath but not completely exhausted.

- Incorporate HIIT intervals 1-2 times per week after warming up.

- Progress workout duration and intensity as your stamina improves.

- Lift weights 2+ days per week for metabolism-boosting muscle retention.

- Focus on different muscle groups (legs, arms, and core) on different days.

Here are some helpful **tips** for getting the most out of your cardio for enhanced fat loss:

- Vary your workouts to prevent plateaus; try new equipment, classes, and videos.

- Train fast in the morning before eating to maximize fat burning.

- Stay hydrated before, during, and after your sessions.

- Listen to motivating music, podcasts, or videos while training.

- Focus on breathing deeply and maintaining good form.

- Cool down and stretch after cardio to aid muscle recovery.

- Refuel within 30–60 minutes with a balanced protein-carb snack.

- Allow at least 1-2 full rest days each week for your body to recover.

Cardiovascular exercise provides enormous benefits beyond just burning calories and fat. It is phenomenal for heart health, building endurance and stamina, reducing stress, and boosting mood. Consistency with your cardio workouts is key; aim to make them a regular habit, like brushing your teeth. Over time, you will see great results in your weight, body composition, energy levels, and overall wellbeing.

High-Intensity Interval Training (HIIT)

High-intensity interval training, or HIIT, has become an incredibly popular and effective exercise strategy for boosting metabolism and promoting fat loss. HIIT involves alternating short bursts of intense cardio exercise with active recovery periods. This type of training torches calories, builds cardiovascular fitness, and triggers excess post-exercise oxygen consumption (EPOC) for enhanced fat burning.

- HIIT workouts manipulate your heart rate by pushing it up near maximum effort during the intense intervals, followed by lowering it during the rest periods. This increase and decrease in heart rate is metabolically demanding. Your body must work extra hard during HIIT, not only to power the intense intervals but also to return your body to homeostasis afterwards.
- This results in a massive calorie burn in a short timeframe. Research indicates HIIT can burn 25–30% more calories compared to other workouts of the same duration. The metabolic benefits of HIIT also extend beyond the training session itself. Studies show a single bout of HIIT can accelerate your metabolism and fat burning for up to 24–48 hours afterwards.
- In addition to major calorie expenditure, HIIT improves the body's ability to utilize fat for fuel. During the high-intensity intervals, your body turns primarily to stored carbs, like glycogen, for immediate energy. But in the recovery segments, your body relies more heavily on fat breakdown to supply your energy needs.
- This greater reliance on fat metabolism carries over even after you finish your workout. Your body becomes more efficient at directing free fatty acids to your muscles to sustain activity and restore glycogen stores. This means that your body will extract more calories from your fat reserves around the clock.
- The intense intervals of HIIT also enhance insulin sensitivity and glucose metabolism. Spikes in intensity trigger the muscles to rapidly take up glucose during the intervals, while the recovery phases allow insulin to do its job of transporting glucose into the muscles effectively. Better glucose management helps reduce fat storage over time.
- In addition to fat-burning effects, HIIT is exceptional for building cardiovascular endurance and strength. The intense intervals stress and strengthen the heart, enhancing its pumping capacity and efficiency. HIIT also builds muscle power and endurance, particularly in the legs, core, and arms, depending on your exercise mode.

To execute an effective HIIT **workout**:

- Warm up for 5–10 minutes to prepare the muscles and heart.

- Alternate 30 second to 2 minute intense intervals with 1-3 minute active rest periods.

- Sustain intervals near max effort (85–95% of max heart rate).

- Include 8–15 total intervals per session (beginners start with fewer).

- Cool down and stretch thoroughly afterwards.

You can tailor HIIT workouts to your personal fitness level and available equipment.

- Sprinting or stair climbing (bodyweight only)

- Kettlebell or dumbbell circuits

- Cycling or rowing machine intervals

- Treadmill power walking on high inclines

- Jumping rope (excellent full-body option)

- Burpees, mountain climbers, and jump squats (no equipment is required).

For best results, incorporate 1-3 HIIT workouts into your weekly exercise routine, in addition to strength training and steady-state cardio. The intense intervals help break plateaus, while the recovery periods allow your body to continually adapt and grow stronger. Take advantage of HIIT's powerful metabolic and cardiovascular benefits to accelerate your fitness and fat loss.

Recovery and Its Importance in Metabolic Health

Exercise and activity are essential components of a healthy metabolism and body weight management. However, the recovery periods between workouts are just as critical for allowing your body to adapt, repair itself, and grow stronger over time. Proper rest and recovery support muscle building, energy levels, hormonal balance, and numerous other factors vital to metabolic health.

- Following intense exercise, microscopic tears and damage occur in muscle fibers, connective tissue, and surrounding structures. The body requires adequate rest to fully repair this damage and synthesize new proteins for building and strengthening muscles. Recovery time also facilitates the restoration of fluids and fuels such as glycogen, as well as the reduction of inflammatory compounds.
- Insufficient recovery can cause subsequent workouts to further degrade the body before it has undergone proper repair. This leads to compromised performance, an increased risk of injury, and lowered metabolism-boosting muscle growth. Ensuring proper recovery allows you to consistently work out with higher quality and intensity.
- In addition to enabling muscle repair, recovery periods give your nervous system a chance to rest and reset after strenuous activity. High-intensity exercise such as weight training, sprinting, and plyometrics substantially tax the central nervous system. Trying to train while fatigued can hinder strength, speed, coordination, and technique. Taking 1-3 rest days between hitting the same major muscle groups facilitates optimal nervous system recovery.
- Adequate recovery also helps maintain beneficial hormone levels related to growth, metabolism, and body composition. Intense workouts cause a temporary spike in catabolic hormones like cortisol that break down tissues. Rest days allow these hormones to return to baseline, enabling greater production of anabolic hormones like testosterone and human growth hormone that build and strengthen muscles.
- Furthermore, getting enough rest helps your immune system stay strong and resilient. Hard training can temporarily suppress immune function, increasing susceptibility to colds and infections. Allowing your body to recover reduces the cumulative immune-suppressing

effects of exercise. Staying healthy enables consistent training with fewer setbacks or sick days that can impede progress.

Here are some **tips** to promote optimal recovery between workouts:

- Take at least one full rest day between intense sessions targeting the same muscle groups. 2+ days is even better.

- Sleep 7-9 hours per night to facilitate tissue repair and refueling.

- Eat a diet high in lean protein.

- Hydrate well by drinking adequate water and electrolytes like sodium and potassium.

- Take an ice bath, use compression wear, or get a massage to aid muscle and joint recovery.

- Go for an easy walk, engage in light stretching, or do foam rolling to boost circulation without overtaxing the body.

- Listen to your body and adjust your training if you feel off or overly fatigued.

- Supplement with anti-inflammatory compounds like omega-3s and curcumin to reduce muscle soreness.

- Avoid alcohol, excess caffeine, and other drugs that interfere with sleep quality and hormone levels.

Recovery is a crucial part of the workout process, not just wasted downtime between training sessions. Properly balancing exercise with rest allows for consistent, high-quality training and peak performance. It also provides metabolic benefits by enabling muscle repair and growth. Make self-care and active recovery practices a regular part of your routine to improve your long-term metabolic health.

Intermittent Fasting and Metabolic Confusion

Intermittent fasting has become an increasingly popular dietary strategy for weight loss and metabolic health. The basic premise involves cycling between periods of fasting and eating, rather than maintaining a constant calorie intake. This approach mimics our evolutionary past, when food was not always readily available. Through intermittent fasting, we activate powerful genetic and metabolic changes that enhance fat burning and preserve muscle mass.

There are several proposed mechanisms by which intermittent fasting benefits metabolic health. During fasting periods, insulin levels drop significantly. This facilitates the release of stored fat for energy. Lower insulin also enhances insulin sensitivity - the cells' ability to respond properly to insulin. This is critical for regulating blood sugar and preventing diabetes. Fasting has also been shown to drive up catecholamines - adrenaline and noradrenaline. These hormones facilitate the utilization of stored body fat for energy.

Some researchers believe intermittent fasting impacts weight loss by reducing overall calorie intake. However, studies show intermittent fasting can boost fat burning even without an overall drop in calories. This suggests a direct metabolic advantage. Fasting periods allow the activation of lipolysis, the breakdown of fat into fatty acids for fuel. This does not occur during a continuous calorie restriction.

There is also evidence that intermittent fasting triggers adaptive cellular repair processes. Autophagy plays a crucial role in recycling damaged cell components. Enhanced autophagy provides anti-aging and disease-prevention effects. It may also contribute to the anti-inflammatory properties of fasting.

Several **methods** of intermittent fasting have emerged, each with varying protocols and benefits. The most common approaches include:

- 16/8 Method - This involves a 16 hour fasting window followed by an 8 hour eating window each day. For example, skipping breakfast and only eating between 12pm and 8pm. This is a simple and sustainable approach.
- 5:2 Diet - This method entails fully fasting or eating just 500-600 calories for 2 nonconsecutive days per week, and eating normally the other 5 days.
- Alternate Day Fasting - Fasting fully or partially every other day. Studies show this can significantly boost fat burning.
- The Warrior Diet - Fast during the day, eat a large meal at night. The daytime fast ranges from 20-22 hours.
- Eat-Stop-Eat - 24 hour fasts 1-2 times per week, remaining days are normal eating.

Regardless of the specific protocol, several **key factors** optimize the effectiveness and safety of an intermittent fasting plan:

- Gradual ramp up - Start with 12-14 hour fasts and slowly progress to longer fasts. This allows the body to adapt and prevents side effects.
- Consume low-carb, high protein and high fiber foods during eating windows - This keeps blood sugar stable, manages hunger and preserves muscle.

- Stay hydrated during fasts with water, herbal tea and coffee.
- Exercise during fasting periods to accelerate fat burning, but limit high-intensity workouts until after you eat.
- Listen to your body and be flexible - Modify or break a fast if you feel unwell.
- Supplement with electrolytes and antioxidants if fasting for extended periods.

The metabolic flexibility induced by intermittent fasting makes it an excellent complement to other diet strategies like carb cycling or calorie cycling. By incorporating occasional fasts or restricting eating to specific windows, you can enhance the fat burning triggered by these calorie-manipulation techniques.

Here is one way to synergistically **combine** intermittent fasting **with carb cycling**:

- Do 24-36 hour fasts 2 times per week - Mondays and Thursdays for example. Drink only water, herbal tea or black coffee during the fasts. You can take 10 grams of branched chain amino acids before and during any workouts.

- On lower carb days, confine meals to an 8 hour eating window like 12pm-8pm. Keep carbs under 50 grams.

- On higher carb days, meals can be eaten over a 10 hour window from 10am-8pm. Get carbs from healthy whole food sources like sweet potatoes, quinoa, fruit etc.

- Take 1-2 rest days per week eating normally without any fasting, carb cycling or calorie targets. Listen to your body.

This integrated approach allows you to enjoy periods of higher carb intake for boosting workout performance and energy levels. But the intermittent fasting and occasional low carb days maximize fat burning, insulin sensitivity and metabolic flexibility. This strategy provides all the benefits of both intermittent fasting and carb/calorie cycling.

Some additional **tips** for maximizing fat loss with this combined approach:

- Engage in high intensity interval training during your fasting state for enhanced fat burning.

- Increase protein intake on fasting and lower carb days to preserve lean muscle mass. Whey protein is ideal.

- Eat lots of non-starchy vegetables, healthy fats and fiber. These help manage hunger.

- Stay hydrated, rest when needed and don't under-eat on non-fasting days.

- Transition slowly, and stick to intermittent fasting frequencies and durations that you can sustain long-term.

The research on intermittent fasting continues to demonstrate powerful benefits for weight control, blood sugar regulation, inflammation reduction and longevity. Combining intermittent fasting with appropriate nutrition and exercise strategies such as carb cycling amplifies the benefits of fat burning and metabolism. Use this integrated, complementary approach to drive robust, lasting improvements in body composition and metabolic health.

Keto Cycling: A Deeper Look

The ketogenic diet has surged in popularity for its ability to drive fat loss, control appetite, optimize brain health, and manage blood sugar levels. This very low-carb, high-fat diet aims to induce a metabolic state of ketosis, where the body switches from using glucose to ketones for fuel. However, long-term strict keto may not be sustainable or ideal for everyone. This is where keto cycling can provide an advantageous alternative.

Keto cycling involves alternating periods of ketogenic dieting with a higher carb intake. This might mean 5-6 days of keto eating followed by 1-2 days of increased carbs. Or even doing daily cyclical keto, where carb sources are strategically consumed around workouts.

There are several proposed **benefits** to cycling in and out of ketosis compared to continuous keto dieting:

- Enhanced athletic performance - Carb loading 1-2 days per week can provide muscles with glycogen to power intense or prolonged workouts.

- Improved metabolic flexibility - The transition between using glucose and ketones for fuel promotes metabolic adaptations.

- Sustainability - Periodic carb refeeds can increase dietary adherence for those who struggle with keto long-term.

- Hormone maintenance - Carb cycling may support thyroid and reproductive hormone function better than strict keto.

- Muscle preservation - Strategic carb intake aids muscle growth and recovery.

The best carb sources for refeed days should primarily be nutritious whole foods like starchy vegetables, legumes, fresh fruit and ancient grains like rice, quinoa and buckwheat. High sugar processed carbs are best avoided.

Protein intake should remain consistent on keto and high carb days. Increased protein aids glycogen restoration and prevents muscle loss when insulin levels spike on high carb days.

Some **supplements** can also optimize keto cycling benefits:

- MCT oil - Provides ketone-generating medium chain fats to support ketosis on low carb days

- Exogenous ketones - Directly supply ketones and accelerate the transition into ketosis during low carb phases.

- Creatine - Enhances strength and muscle-building during workout and high carb days.

- Beta-alanine - Increases muscle endurance capacity when carbing up.

- Greens powder - Boosts micronutrients on all days for optimal health.

Here are some keto cycling **protocols** to consider:

5 Low/2 High

- Follow standard keto diet guidelines for 5 days - under 50g net carbs, adequate protein and high fat.

- On 2 consecutive high carb days, increase carbs to 100-150g, coming mainly from nutrient-dense sources.

- Fasting for 12-16 hours overnight can help prime the transition back into ketosis after carb loading.

Daily Cyclical Keto

- Consume under 30g net carbs for all meals except pre and post workout.

- Ingest 30-60g fast-digesting carbs like dextrose or white rice 30 minutes before workouts.

- Eat another 30-60g carbohydrates immediately after training.

- Ketone supplements can expedite the reentry into ketosis between workouts.

Targeted Cyclical Keto

- Remain in ketosis with under 30g net carbs daily.

- Only increase carbs around select low-intensity or skill-based workouts by having 30-40g 15-30 minutes pre-workout.

- Limit high carb days to only 1-2 times per week maximum.

You can also incorporate cyclical keto strategies into other well-known diet plans:

- Keto-Paleo Hybrid - Do keto 5 days, higher carb paleo 2 days. Emphasize vegetables, fruit and tubers for carb sources.
- Carb Backloading - Restrict carbs until post-workout evening meals on some training days.
- Intermittent Fasting Keto - Fast morning and midday, consume carbs at night on high days.

When transitioning out of ketosis to higher carb intake, expect a rapid increase in weight due to muscle glycogen restoration, intestinal contents and state changes. This is just water weight and will drop again within 1-3 days of lowering carbs.

Some **tips** for making keto cycling more effective:

- Match carb intake on high days to activity demands - If training hard and heavy, increase carbs; if inactive, limit intake.

- Time carb intake optimally - Focus high carb meals around exercise for muscle glycogen needs.

- Prevent fat adaptation plateaus - Periodically cycle calories in addition to carbs.

- Include nutritious, fiber-rich carbs - Slow burning complex carbs are best for workout fuel and health.

Keto cycling provides a compelling middle ground between strict ketogenic dieting and higher carb intake patterns. When executed strategically, it allows you to reap the advantages of carbohydrates and ketosis within a customizable framework that aligns with your goals and preferences. Use these protocols and tips to harness the performance enhancing and physique boosting potential of carb cycling.

Plant-Based Approaches to Metabolic Confusion

A whole food, plant-based diet can provide a nutritious and sustainable approach to enhancing metabolic flexibility. With careful planning, vegetarian and vegan eating patterns can meet protein needs while supporting fat loss and muscle building goals. The key is to strategically incorporate variety and use certain food combinations to optimize absorption.

Protein is a critical macronutrient for preserving or building lean muscle mass while in a calorie deficit. Without adequate protein intake, metabolic slowdown can occur and more muscle may be catabolized for fuel. To obtain sufficient protein on a plant-based diet, you can:

- Legumes - Beans, lentils, peas. For complete proteins, it is best to eat with grains.

- Soy foods - Tofu, tempeh, edamame. Provide complete proteins.

- Seitan - Wheat gluten protein with a meat-like texture. Can be seasoned in different ways.

- Nutritional yeast - Inactivated yeast flakes with B vitamins and protein. Use on salads, soups, pasta.

- Nuts and seeds - Especially hemp, pumpkin, chia, flax, almonds. Blend into smoothies.

- Ancient grains - Quinoa, amaranth, farro. Mix with legumes for full amino acid profile.

- Green peas - A protein-rich vegetable consumed on its own or in dishes.

- Protein powders - Pea, hemp, rice or soy powders can supplement diet as needed.

It is wise to consume a protein source with each meal and snack. Varying plant proteins day to day enhances overall amino acid diversity. A general protein target to support metabolic goals is 0.5-0.7g per pound of body weight. Those lifting heavy weights may need up to 1g per pound.

In addition to adequate protein, the right balance of **carbohydrates** is key for optimizing body composition. Here are effective plant-based approaches:

- Time carb intake - Eat most carbs post-workout to maximize utilization and minimize fat storage. Avoid carbs at night.

- Cycle high/low carb days - Lower carb days enhance fat burning periods. Higher carb days replenish muscle glycogen.

- Combine proteins and carbs - Eating legumes, quinoa or buckwheat with veggies balances meal nutrition.

- Choose low glycemic carbs - Go for steel cut oats, lentils, chickpeas, sweet potatoes. These provide sustained energy.

- Load up on non-starchy veggies - Broccoli, spinach, kale, peppers, mushrooms etc. Provide nutrients without carbohydrate overload.

Healthy fats should not be neglected for hormone balance, brain health and antioxidant support. Excellent vegan fat sources include:

- Nuts and seeds - Walnuts, almonds, pecans, chia and flax.

- Nut/seed butters - Look for options with minimal added oils.

- Avocados - Nutrient rich with beneficial monounsaturated fats.

- Olives and olive oil - Heart healthy antioxidant fats.

- Coconut oil/milk - Contains medium chain triglycerides for energy.

- Dark chocolate - Provides antioxidant flavonoids plus fat.

- Tofu/tempeh - Good sources of omega-3 alpha-linolenic acid.

Here are some sample plant-based **meal plans** applying the metabolic confusion principles:

Lower Carb Day

- Breakfast - Tofu veggie scramble with kale and nutritional yeast
- Lunch - Lentil walnut taco salad with greens
- Dinner - Veggie curry with paneer (tofu) and cauliflower rice
- Snacks - Green smoothie with hemp protein, celery sticks with almond butter

Higher Carb Day

- Breakfast - Overnight oats with blueberries, flax and almond milk
- Lunch - Burrito bowl with black beans, rice, salsa and guacamole
- Dinner - Thai peanut tempeh stir fry with quinoa
- Snacks - Plantain chips with guacamole, mixed berries

In addition to nutrition, optimizing workout timing and recovery is key. Avoid intense cardio exercise while fasting. Do cardio after weights or meal, utilizing carb intake for performance. Proper rest and sleep are critical for plant-based athletes' metabolic health.

Supplements like creatine monohydrate, vitamin B12 and potentially EPA/DHA omega-3s can provide insurance for those following a strictly plant-based diet.

At the end of the day, a whole food plant-based approach centered around vegetables, legumes, nuts/seeds, whole grains and fruit can certainly support muscle retention and fat loss goals. With adequate protein at each meal, carb cycling, strategic meal timing and planned supplementation, plant-based metabolic confusion diets can be safe and effective.

Supplements: Do They Help?

The supplement industry rakes in billions of dollars annually marketing powders, pills, and potions that promise to accelerate fat loss, amplify muscle growth, and optimize human performance. With so many products on the market making seemingly miraculous claims, it can be tempting to want to try them all. But do supplements really enhance the results of your metabolic flexibility program? The truth lies somewhere in the middle. Not all supplements live up to the hype, but certain strategic additions can provide benefits.

When it comes to **fat loss**, one of the most popular supplement categories are thermogenics which are compounds claimed to boost metabolism and increase calorie burn. These can include stimulants like caffeine, green tea extract, synephrine and yohimbine. Some evidence suggests that when taken pre-workout, these may help mobilize more stored fat and blunt appetite. However, effects are often minor and side effects like jitteriness can occur if dosing is too high. Non-stimulant agents like L-carnitine, CLA and fucoxanthin have limited research support for fat loss at this point.

Perhaps the most effective legal OTC fat burning supplements are ECA stacks - ephedrine, caffeine and aspirin. This combination taps into the thermogenic power of caffeine and ephedrine. But safety issues exist with ephedrine, making the risk-reward profile questionable. Overall, fat burners can provide a modest enhancement, but are not necessary and work best alongside a consistent diet and exercise.

What about **muscle building** supplements like creatine and beta-alanine? These do have more substantial evidence behind their efficacy. Creatine supplements help increase strength and power output by maximizing muscular phosphocreatine stores. Beta-alanine reduces fatigue during intense anaerobic exercise by boosting muscle carnosine levels. Both are worth considering for boosting high intensity workout capacity. Citrulline is another solid pre-workout choice for increasing exercise endurance and muscle pumps by optimizing nitric oxide synthesis. Post-workout, whey protein is ideal for providing muscles's needed amino acids.

Certain compounds can optimize **body composition** during low carb or ketogenic dieting phases. MCT oil and exogenous ketones like BHB salts can provide supplemental ketone energy. This enhances cognition and workout capacity when limiting carbs. EAAs or branched chain amino acids taken pre or post training can preserve muscle while in ketosis. Electrolytes like sodium, potassium and magnesium should also be replenished when transitioning into a low carb state.

What about **testosterone** boosters and **pro-hormones**? Despite lofty marketing claims, most natural T-boosters do not significantly increase testosterone because they rely on weak herbs such as tribulus and DHEA. Pro-hormones were essentially banned in 2005. Safer options for boosting testosterone include weight training, adequate sleep, stress management and potentially zinc or vitamin D supplementation.

Beyond direct performance enhancement, certain supplements **provide key micronutrients** that support metabolic health:

- Probiotics - Boost healthy gut bacteria populations, which influence digestion, immunity and inflammation.

- Omega-3 fish oils - Powerful anti-inflammatory; may enhance fat loss and insulin sensitivity.

- Vitamin D - Many are deficient; aids neuromuscular function and overall health.

- Magnesium - Improves sleep quality and muscle recovery.

- Greens powders - Alkalizing; provide antioxidant fruits and vegetables.

The smartest supplement strategy is to focus on the basics - quality whey protein, creatine, caffeine, citrulline, vitamin D, probiotics, and fish oil offer the biggest bang for your buck. Avoid getting caught up in exotic herbs, uncomfortable stimulants or questionable pro-hormone derivatives. As always, dial in your nutrition, training and lifestyle first before turning to supplements for that extra one percent edge.

Seasonal and Local Eating Habits

Eating locally and seasonally sourced whole foods provides a natural form of metabolic confusion. Following the yearly ebb and flow of produce availability challenges the body with an ever-changing palette of phytonutrients, vitamins, and minerals. This complements the metabolic flexibility diet's intentional nutrition cycling.

Eating seasonally means filling your plate primarily with fruits and vegetables that are currently in harvest. In the summer, feast on berries, stone fruits, tomatoes, leafy greens, corn, zucchini, and more. As fall approaches, emphasize apples, pears, squash, sweet potatoes, cauliflower, and mushrooms. In winter, citrus fruits, root veggies, cabbage, kale, and broccoli flourish. Come spring, enjoy the bounty of peas, asparagus, spinach, cherries, and artichokes.

Aligning your eating patterns with seasonal harvests provides several **advantages**:

- Higher nutrient levels - Produce picked ripe contains more antioxidants and phytochemicals. These start to decline after harvest.

- Better taste - Fruit allowed to fully ripen on the vine or tree develops optimal sweetness and flavor.

- Environmental sustainability - Minimizes the need for long distance transport, refrigeration and storage.

- Supports local farmers - Purchasing through seasonal farmer's markets provides income for small farms.

- Cost savings - Seasonal items are plentiful and inexpensive during peak harvest periods.

- Inspires variety - Enjoying the ever-changing produce landscape keeps meals exciting and diverse.

In addition to eating seasonally, prioritizing locally grown food options also confers health and **environmental** upsides:

- Maximal nutrients - The less time between farm and table, the more nutrients remain intact.

- Reduces fossil fuel use - Food traveling thousands of miles burns more oil and emits carbon.

- Strengthens community - Face-to-face farmer markets foster connections.

- Builds regional food security - Increases resilience if large supply chains are disrupted.

- Benefits local economy - Supports family farms and food artisans in your area.

Here are some **tips** for shifting towards seasonal, local eating:

- Shop at farmers markets - Chat with producers and ask for recommendations.

- Join a CSA program - Receive weekly boxes of seasonal items from local farms.

- Read up on seasonal charts - Learn when key produce is at peak availability.

- Visit pick-your-own farms - Gather berries, tree fruit and other crops straight from the source.

- Try new seasonal recipes - Search for ideas online or in cookbooks tailored to the season.

- Freeze or can surplus seasonal bounty - Stock up on veggies when abundant for use later in the year.

- Start your own garden - Grow a portion of your own seasonal fruits, vegetables and herbs.

- Let seasons guide your menu - Construct meals around fresh seasonal ingredients.

- Preserve nutrients and taste - Cook produce minimally using gentle methods like steaming.

Here is a sample **meal plan** for seasonal metabolic confusion:

Spring

- Breakfast - Asparagus and leek frittata
- Lunch - Mixed greens salad with strawberries, almonds, chèvre
- Dinner - Pan seared salmon with dill, roasted artichokes

Summer

- Breakfast - Seasonal fruit salad, pistachio mint yogurt
- Lunch - Arugula salad with grilled peaches, tomatoes, burrata
- Dinner - Grilled shrimp skewers with corn, zucchini

Fall

- Breakfast - Maple cinnamon apple oatmeal
- Lunch - Roasted beets, carrots, chickpeas over spinach
- Dinner - Turkey meatballs with butternut squash noodles

Winter

- Breakfast - Veggie hash with sweet potato, Brussels sprouts
- Lunch - Cauliflower soup, sourdough bread
- Dinner - Braised short ribs, parsnip mash, Swiss chard

Aligning your nutrition efforts with the natural seasonal rhythms of agriculture provides a synergistic enhancement to metabolic health. Vary your plate throughout the year for diverse phytonutrients. When in doubt, remember that nature knows best.

CHAPTER 6: MASTERING CARB CYCLING FOR METABOLIC

ENHANCEMENT

Understanding Carb Cycling: Basics and Benefits

Carb cycling is a nutritional strategy that involves deliberately manipulating carbohydrate intake on a regular schedule. Carb cycling, also known as nutrient timing, aims to match periods of high and low carb intake with your body's needs on training and rest days.

When done correctly, carb cycling offers numerous benefits. It can speed up fat loss while preserving lean muscle mass. It provides fuel for intense training while facilitating recovery on off days. Carb cycling enhances metabolic flexibility—the body's ability to switch between using carbs or fats for energy. With greater metabolic flexibility, you can tap into fat stores more efficiently when carbs are low while still utilizing carbs effectively on high-carb days.

Carb cycling basics

To understand carb cycling, it helps to recognize that not all carbohydrates are created equal. We categorize carbs based on their glycemic index, which determines how quickly they raise blood sugar levels after eating. Low-glycemic carbs break down more slowly, offering sustained energy. High glycemic carbs cause rapid spikes in blood sugar that soon crash.

Another key factor is carb timing—when you eat carbs relative to exercise. After a workout, muscles store carbs as glycogen instead of body fat. The strategic use of low and high glycemic carbs at specific times optimizes workout performance, recovery, and body composition.

Setting up a carb cycling plan requires determining your total calorie needs and meal frequency. You'll designate high-carb, moderate-carb, and low-carb intake days based on your training schedule. High-carb days match up with the most intense workout days, while low-carb days fall on rest days.

A typical cycle lasts one week, but the exact frequency and ratio of high and low carb days can vary based on goals, activity levels, and individual responses. Many plans include 2-3 high-carb days, 2-3 moderate-carb days, and 1-2 low-carb days per week.

Carb cycling benefits

Carb cycling offers many benefits, including:

- Enhanced fat burning: lower carb intake prompts your body to tap into fat stores. Cycling carbs prevents the metabolic slowdown associated with extended low-carb diets.

- Fuel for exercise: timed high-carb meals provide energy for challenging workouts and replenish glycogen stores needed for performance.

- Appetite control: Balancing high- and low-carb days helps manage hunger and cravings.

- Greater muscle gains: Spiking insulin with high carbohydrate intake around workouts promotes efficient nutrient delivery for building and repairing muscle.

- Improved insulin sensitivity: Varying carb intake prevents chronically elevated insulin from excessive carb consumption.

- Increased dietary flexibility: carb cycling allows room for a wider range of foods and prevents feeling deprived.

- Better energy and focus: stable blood sugar levels translate to fewer energy crashes and mental fog.

- Sustainable long-term plan: The built-in variety of carb cycling enhances adherence for lasting results.

While the benefits are substantial, carb cycling is not advisable for everyone. Individuals managing diabetes or on specific medications should consult their healthcare provider before modifying their carbohydrate intake. Tracking macros accurately is required for the best outcomes. Carb cycling also involves more planning and preparation compared to a standard diet.

Structuring a Carb Cycling Program: High and Low Days

When setting up a carb cycling plan, one of the most important considerations is properly structuring your high- and low-carb days. This involves determining the right calorie and macro ratio splits for both types of days and aligning them strategically with your training schedule. By thoughtfully planning high- and low-carb days, you can maximize carb cycling benefits while also ensuring the diet is sustainable long-term.

- Total calorie intake is the foundation of any carb cycling program. Begin by estimating your maintenance calories—the amount you need to maintain your current weight. Factor in your basal metabolic rate, activity levels, and weight goals. Reduce total calories by 10–20% on low-carb days for a moderate deficit that spurs fat loss. Keep calories closer to maintenance on high-carb days to support training and recovery.
- The macronutrient ratio of carbs, protein, and fat will differ on high versus low days. On high-carb days, carbs will account for 50–60% of total calories. Get the majority of carbs from nutrient-dense, low-glycemic sources like fruits, vegetables, whole grains, and legumes. Include 20–30% of calories from protein to build and repair muscle. The remaining 15-20% should come from healthy fats like olive oil, nuts, seeds, and fatty fish.
- In contrast, carb intake on low days will be cut approximately in half—down to just 25–35% of total calories. Offset this by increasing healthy fats to 40–50% of calories on low-carb days. Also emphasize plenty of lean protein sources like chicken, turkey, fish, eggs, and Greek yogurt. Protein should remain consistent at 20–30% of calories, whether on high- or low-carb days.
- The weekly cadence of high- and low-carb days depends on your training schedule. Schedule the most high-carb days when you have intense workouts to fuel performance and recovery. Follow resistance training sessions with a high-carb day to replenish glycogen and spike insulin for muscle growth.
- Place low-carb days on off days or light cardio sessions. Your body can tap into fat without compromising low-intensity activities. Avoid carb restriction on consecutive days; cycle

between high and low days to maximize metabolic flexibility. If following a 3-day high, 2-day low pattern, avoid low-carb days back-to-back.

Here is an **example** of a carb cycling plan layout with three high-carb days and two low-carb days:

Monday: High (resistance training)
Tuesday: Low (rest)
Wednesday: High (HIIT)
Thursday: Low (light cardio)
Friday: High (resistance training)
Saturday: Low (rest)
Sunday: Moderate carb refeed

This schedule ensures adequate fuel on the most demanding workout days while facilitating fat burning on off days. To avoid a metabolic slowdown, the weekly refeed replenishes glycogen stores. Add or reduce high- and low-carb days based on your goals and schedule. The optimal carb cycling split will take some trial and error.

Make carb cycling more manageable. Batch cook proteins, grains, and carb sources such as quinoa or sweet potatoes. Having prepared ingredients makes assembling meals simple. Rely on nutrient-dense whole foods instead of processed low-carb replacements.

With diligent tracking of macros, strategic structuring of high and low days, and advance meal prep, carb cycling can be incorporated as a nutrition plan for the long haul. Just be prepared to make adjustments over time based on changes in training volume, muscle gain goals, and weekly progress.

Timing Carb Intake for Optimal Performance

Proper timing of carbohydrate intake around exercise is critical for optimizing workout performance and recovery. The key is to coordinate your carbohydrate consumption with your body's needs at different stages. Thoughtful carb timing will provide energy during intense sessions, minimize fat storage, and speed up post-workout recovery.

The basics of carb timing involve eating carbs in the hours before exercise to load muscles with glycogen. During longer endurance training, carbs help maintain blood glucose and spare glycogen stores. Consuming carbs immediately after a workout quickly restores glycogen depleted by exercise. It is ideal to adjust carb timing for different types, durations, and intensities of training.

Pre-workout carb timing

For most moderate-to-high-intensity training lasting over an hour, aim for a pre-workout meal 2-4 hours beforehand containing 1-4 grams of carbs per kg of bodyweight. Stick to low-glycemic carbs like oats, whole-grain bread, or beans, which provide steady energy. The closer your pre-workout meal is to exercise, opt for lighter and more rapidly digesting carbs such as fruit, rice cakes, or low-fat yogurt. Avoid fat and fiber near exercise, as this slows digestion. Stay hydrated before training, and sip electrolyte drinks to maintain energy.

During longer endurance activities like marathons, consuming 30–60 grams of carbs per hour can significantly boost performance. Rapidly digested options like sports drinks, gels, chews, and beans supply energy to the working muscles. Don't dramatically increase carbohydrate intake beyond what your body can utilize to avoid gastric distress.

Post-workout carb timing

After training, the 2-hour anabolic window is prime time for carbohydrate consumption to optimally refuel glycogen stores. Aim for 0.5–1 gram of carbs per kg of bodyweight within the first 30 minutes post-exercise, and repeat with a meal again 1-2 hours later. The fastest-digesting carbs, like dextrose or white bread, can spike insulin most effectively during this phase. Combine these carbs with a source of protein to aid in muscle repair and growth.

On lower-carb days, limit post-workout carbs and rely more on protein and fat. Still, some fast-digesting carbs pre- and post-exercise, even on low-carb days, provide fuel for the demands of training while keeping carbs in check on rest days.

Carb type and timing recommendations can also vary based on the **goal** of a given training session.

Strength training:

- Pre-workout: 1-2 grams/kg of low-glycemic carbs 2-3 hours prior to lifting

- When drinking branched-chain amino acid (BCAA),

- Post-workout: 0.5–1 gram/kg of high-glycemic carbs and 20–40 grams of protein within 45 minutes

Endurance training:

- Pre-workout: 1-4 grams/kg of low-glycemic carbs 2-4 hours prior

- 30–60 grams of mostly glucose-based fuel every 45–60 minutes

- Post-workout: 0.5–1 gram/kg of high-glycemic carbs and 20–40 grams of protein within 45 minutes

HIIT (high-intensity interval training):

- Pre-workout: carbs that are easily digested, like fruit, 30 to 60 minutes prior

- During: Not needed due to session brevity

- Post-workout: 0.5–1 gram/kg of high-glycemic carbs and 20–40 grams of protein within 30 minutes

The trickiest part of timing carbs for performance is the inevitable trial and error to determine what works optimally for your body and your chosen training. Pay close attention to how you feel during workouts when making even small tweaks to carb timing. Maintain a consistent protocol for a minimum of 2-3 weeks to evaluate the need for adjustments.

With diligent training logs and being in tune with your body, you can leverage proper carb timing as a key strategy for getting the most out of your workouts and recovery.

Carb Cycling and Its Impact on Fat Loss

When it comes to achieving sustainable fat loss, few nutrition strategies are as effective as carb cycling. Manipulating carbohydrate intake through strategic high and low carb days accelerates the fat burning process by optimizing hormones, energy balance, and workout performance. Implemented properly, carb cycling kickstarts impressive reductions in body fat while maintaining precious lean muscle.

Understanding the mechanisms by which carb cycling enhances fat loss is key to maximizing results. By fluctuating carbohydrate intake, the body never adapts to a set point that slows metabolism over time. The ongoing flux keeps the body guessing and responsive. On high-carb days, insulin sensitivity remains high, shuttling nutrients into muscles efficiently. Low-carb days help regulate appetite hormones, control cravings, and teach the body to utilize fat for fuel.

This enhanced metabolic flexibility allows your body to switch seamlessly between burning carbs or fats for energy. With carb cycling, you get the benefits of a low-carb diet on off days with the performance-boosting perks of adequate carb intake on workout days. This best-of-both-worlds setup creates the optimal environment for losing fat.

Carb cycling also promotes fat loss through energy balance manipulation. On reduced-carb days, calories are naturally decreased without actively cutting them. You simply reduce portions of energy-dense carbs, which lowers overall calories. This slight deficit is enough to nudge fat loss forward. High-carb days at maintenance calories prevent the adaptive slowdown of standard dieting.

Additionally, carb cycling lets you put calorie surplus to better use compared to a traditional high-carb diet. The strategic timing of extra carbs to fuel tough workouts partitions more of those calories toward performance and recovery rather than excess storage as fat.

Several fat-loss-specific **benefits** arise from carb cycling:

- Lower insulin levels on low-carb days enable greater lipolysis—the breakdown of fat for energy. Stable blood glucose and insulin levels also reduce fat storage.

- Appetite regulation is improved on reduced-carb days, allowing easier compliance with calorie targets.

- Including an occasional refeed or higher carb day boosts leptin levels, spurring the metabolism to continue burning fat.

- Carb cycling provides dietary flexibility. No food groups are completely off limits, which supports long-term compliance.

- Timed carbs around workouts enhance intensity. Burning more calories during exercise directly aids fat loss results.

- Strategic carb consumption optimizes hormone balance. Cortisol is reduced, while testosterone and growth hormone are elevated.

- Preserving and building muscle through properly fueled training increases the resting metabolic rate, which passively burns more calories.

As with any nutrition approach, individual tweaking is required to maximize fat loss from carb cycling. Training status, lean mass, insulin sensitivity, and carbohydrate tolerance can all have an impact on appropriate macro amounts and high/low day frequency. Be prepared to experiment and track data consistently.

If properly integrated into your lifestyle and training regimen, carb cycling can produce remarkable fat-loss outcomes. Cycling high- and low-carb days is a proven way to shed stubborn body fat while retaining hard-earned muscle.

Common Mistakes and How to Avoid Them

When implementing a carb cycling plan, mistakes and missteps can hamper your progress. Knowing the most common carb cycling errors and how to sidestep them will help you achieve success faster. You can seamlessly incorporate carb cycling into your lifestyle with some education on potential pitfalls.

1. One of the biggest mistakes is taking a haphazard approach without tracking macros. Guesstimating portions and not counting grams of carbs, protein, and fat consumed each day makes it impossible to adhere to your high and low carb targets. Get in the habit of weighing foods and logging meals, especially when first starting out. With time, visually estimating serving sizes gets easier.
2. Insufficient calories on reduced-carb days can also backfire. Too steep of a calorie deficit prompts the body to conserve energy, stalling weight loss. Get aggressive only on your carb reduction, keep protein adequate, and ensure overall calories on low days are appropriate for your needs. The scale may temporarily plateau, but metabolic slowdown will be avoided.
3. Not adjusting your workout routine is another misstep. Low-carb days necessitate reduced-intensity cardio sessions versus intense HIIT-style training optimized for higher carb intake. Don't try to maintain the same training volumes regardless of your macrocycle. Sync your workouts to match low- or high-carb days.
4. Avoid getting stuck by always following a rigid high- or low-day pattern. Your exact carb needs may vary over time. Remain flexible and make changes based on your progress. For instance, incorporate an extra-high-carb day if you experience low energy during workouts, indicating inadequate fuel.

Further **mistakes** to sidestep include:

- Spiking insulin too frequently can hinder fat burning. Ensure adequate time between carb-heavy meals for blood sugar to stabilize.

- Overdoing unhealthy fats like fried foods, excess red meat, and high-fat dairy products on low-carb days. Focus on healthy, unsaturated fats.

- Not eating enough fiber when increasing carbs. Focus on nutrient-dense, high-fiber carbohydrate sources.

- Letting protein intake drift too low on reduced-carb days. Make protein a priority, regardless of cutting carbs.

- Eliminating carb cycling completely once you've lost the target amount of weight or body fat. Maintaining carb cycling as an eating style sustains the metabolic benefits.

- Resuming poor snacking habits on high-carb days. Just because you can eat more carbs doesn't mean you should overdo the junk food.

The most effective way to prevent carb cycling mistakes is to be prepared. Make sure you understand the principles behind carb cycling before diving in. Plan out weekly menus and meal prep. Have healthy snacks like nuts, Greek yogurt, and hard-boiled eggs readily available to mitigate hunger on low days.

Accept that trial and error will be part of the process. Track data consistently and tweak your macros gradually over time. Remain hyper-focused when ramping up carb intake to channel surplus calories into muscle growth rather than haphazard fat storage.

Be kind to yourself if you slip up or struggle at times adjusting to the carb cycling regimen. Refocus and get back on track at your next meal. With increased knowledge, vigilance, and practice, carb cycling can transform your physique without major hurdles.

Long-Term Management and Adjustments in Carb Cycling

The metabolic and physique-enhancing benefits of carb cycling make it an ideal long-term eating strategy. However, sustainability requires making smart adjustments over time as your body, performance goals, and schedule change. Make a commitment to continuous monitoring, evaluation, and adaptability to ensure that carb cycling remains an optimal lifestyle choice.

- After the initial ramp-up phase of establishing your carb cycling baseline, reassess your progress weekly. Take body measurements and photos to tangibly track fat loss and muscle growth. Log workouts to gauge if strength or endurance gains are plateauing. Evaluate energy levels, hunger, cravings, and mood to determine if macro amounts and meal timing need refinement.
- Be prepared to gradually alter your high- and low-day carbohydrate intake and calorie targets as needed. Your carb tolerance and needs will likely change. As you build muscle and your metabolism increases, you may require more overall calories or higher carb days to fuel new growth. If fat loss slows, consider adding an extra low-carb day or incrementally reducing daily carbohydrate grams.
- Additionally, high- and low-carbohydrate needs often vary seasonally. In more active summer months, your training intensity can necessitate additional high-carb days. During the winter, when less active, lowering the average carbohydrate intake accelerates fat burning. Remain vigilant, adjusting as conditions change.

Here are a few **signs** that it may be time to change your carb cycling approach:

- Fat loss plateaus
- Decreased workout performance
- Increased hunger and cravings
- Inability to gain or maintain muscle
- Low energy, fatigue, and brain fog
- Insomnia or sleep issues
- Stalled strength or endurance gains
- Weight fluctuations greater than 2–3 pounds

To spur ongoing progress, periodically experiment with **changes** such as:

- Altering your high/low day carb ratio
- Shifting meal frequency and timing
- Adding HIIT sessions on low days
- Increasing protein intake
- Reducing portion sizes of unhealthy carbs
- Utilizing post-workout supplements like protein or creatine
- Scheduling an extended "diet break" at maintenance calories

Avoid drastic modifications like suddenly removing high-carb days for an extended period. Make small, incremental changes to allow your body to adapt while still promoting fat burning and muscle growth. Be extremely patient; carb cycling improvements often unfold slowly over many months. Trust the process and stay consistent.

For long-term sustainability, integrate occasional higher-carb refeed meals. This provides mental relief, boosts leptin, and prevents metabolic adaptation. Time refeeds strategically, like the night before an intense workout, to fuel performance.

To simplify carb cycling, rotate the same meals on a regular basis. Get proficient at meal-prepping several staple high- and low-carb meals for efficient execution. To support adherence, keep a variety of food choices within your macro parameters.

You can maintain carb cycling as an optimal eating strategy for physique goals and overall health for years with mindful tracking and responsive tweaking. Consistency, data-driven adjustments, and flexibility are key to making carb cycling work over the long run.

CHAPTER 7: LIFESTYLE FACTORS IMPACTING METABOLISM

Sleep and Metabolic Health

Getting enough quality sleep is crucial for maintaining a healthy metabolism and promoting weight loss. Unfortunately, many people struggle to get the recommended 7-9 hours of sleep per night. Chronic sleep deprivation can wreak havoc on your metabolic health in numerous ways.

In the short term, skimping on sleep causes an imbalance in **key hunger hormones**. Levels of the appetite-suppressing hormone leptin drop, while levels of the hunger hormone ghrelin rise. This fuels cravings, especially for high-calorie foods. Just one night of limited sleep can boost calorie intake by up to 500 calories the following day. Over time, these extra calories lead to weight gain. Sleep deprivation also impairs glucose metabolism. Insufficient sleep causes insulin resistance, raising blood sugar levels. High blood sugar triggers increased calorie intake and fat storage.

Sleep loss also stimulates the **sympathetic nervous system**, increasing blood pressure and stress hormone production. Cortisol promotes fat storage in the abdomen. There is also a reduction in growth hormone, which is crucial for burning fat. Melatonin, which helps regulate metabolism, also decreases.

Furthermore, being tired all the time decreases **motivation** for physical activity. You're more likely to skip workouts, take the elevator instead of the stairs, or just remain sedentary. Reduced activity translates to fewer calories burned over the course of a day. Exhaustion also negatively impacts strength training and muscle repair. Muscle loss slows metabolism further.

Aim for 7-9 hours of quality sleep per night to keep your metabolism optimized. Here are some **tips**:

- Stick to consistent bed and wake times, even on weekends. This strengthens the body's natural circadian rhythms.

- Avoid screens and bright lights before bedtime. Blue-light exposure suppresses melatonin. Read a book or take a bath instead.

- Cut off eating 2-3 hours before bed. Allow time to digest. Refrain from alcohol, caffeine, and spicy foods at night, as these can disrupt sleep.

- Make sure your bedroom is cool, dark, and quiet. Blackout curtains or a sleep mask help block light. Consider a white noise machine to muffle sounds.

- Establish a relaxing pre-bed routine, like light stretches or meditation. It signals to the body and brain that it's time to wind down.

- Limit daytime naps to 30 minutes or less. Longer naps interfere with the nighttime sleep drive.

- Manage stress through techniques like deep breathing, yoga, or journaling during the day. Don't go to bed anxious.

- If you suspect a sleep disorder, such as insomnia or apnea, see your doctor. Treatments can improve the quality of sleep.

Optimizing sleep enhances metabolic functioning, allowing your body to work at peak efficiency. You'll feel more energized for activity and less prone to cravings. Plus, growth and fat-burning hormones remain balanced. Making sleep a priority is one of the most effective tools for sustainable weight management.

Stress Management Techniques

Stress is an inevitable part of life. But when it becomes chronic, it can wreak havoc on your health and metabolism. Stress prompts the body to produce high levels of cortisol and other hormones that lead to inflammation, blood sugar dysregulation, increased belly fat storage, and suppressed immunity. Learning to properly manage stress is critical for maintaining metabolic flexibility.

1. Start by identifying your main stressors. Common triggers include work pressures, financial issues, relationship conflicts, poor time management, negative self-talk, and a lack of work-life balance. You may not be able to eliminate all sources of stress, but recognizing the primary culprits is the first step toward better management.
2. Next, build your resilience through daily relaxation practices. Simple, deep breathing for just 5–10 minutes helps trigger the relaxation response, lowering the heart rate and blood pressure. Try inhaling deeply through the nose, holding for a few seconds, and exhaling slowly through the mouth. Visualization, mindfulness meditation, yoga, and tai chi are other excellent options for effective stress relief.
3. Engage in moderate aerobic exercise like walking, cycling, or swimming for at least 30 to 60 minutes per day. Cardiovascular activity stimulates the production of endorphins, the body's feel-good hormones. It also improves sleep quality, mood, and energy levels. Strength training, 2-3 days per week, is beneficial as well.
4. Make time for leisure activities you enjoy, such as reading, crafting, playing sports, hiking, or listening to music. Do things that provide a mental break, stimulate your creativity, or make you laugh. Focus on positive outlets that enhance your overall wellbeing. Don't rely on unhealthy habits like smoking, drinking excess alcohol, or emotional eating for coping.
5. Improve your time management skills to avoid feeling overwhelmed. Prioritize important tasks, delegate when possible, limit distractions, and break large projects into manageable chunks. Also, build time buffers into your schedule. Rushing creates more stress.
6. Watch out for negative thought patterns like catastrophizing or self-criticism. Instead, reframe situations in a more positive light. Look for opportunities to learn and grow. Be compassionate and encourage yourself. Surround yourself with positive social support.
7. Make sure you get adequate sleep, hydrate properly, and eat a balanced diet. Your body is less equipped to handle stress when running on little rest, dehydration, and nutritional deficiencies. Take steps to support your physical health.
8. Consider therapies like massage, acupuncture, music, or art therapy to aid relaxation. If you continue struggling with stress, seek counseling. A professional can help you gain perspective and teach healthy coping strategies tailored to your situation.

Learning to manage stress takes commitment and practice. But the payoff is huge in terms of enhancing metabolic flexibility, promoting weight loss, and reducing disease risk. By making stress management a regular habit, you'll put yourself in a better position to achieve optimal health.

The Role of Gut Health

Your gastrointestinal system plays a major role in metabolic health. The gut microbiome—the complex community of trillions of bacteria residing in your digestive tract—has a powerful influence on weight management. Optimizing your gut health through diet, lifestyle choices, and targeted supplements can enhance fat burning and reduce obesity risk.

A diverse, balanced microbiome promotes the production of short-chain fatty acids and other compounds that regulate appetite, glucose tolerance, and fat storage. Beneficial gut bacteria also support immune function, reduce inflammation, and improve digestive motility. On the other hand, an imbalanced microbiome leads to increased intestinal permeability ("leaky gut"), nutrient malabsorption, inflammation, insulin resistance, and fat accumulation.

Several factors contribute to poor gut health. Diets high in processed foods, sugar, and unhealthy fats alter the microbiome by promoting the growth of harmful bacteria. Lack of plant fiber starves good bacteria of their preferred "prebiotic" fuel. Chronic stress, inadequate sleep, and antibiotic overuse also disrupt microbial balance. Obesity and weight gain are associated with dysbiosis.

Fortunately, you can cultivate a healthy microbiome through **diet** and **lifestyle** interventions. Eat plenty of fiber-rich fruits, vegetables, whole grains, legumes, nuts, and seeds. These provide prebiotics that selectively feed beneficial bacteria. Fermented foods like yogurt, kefir, sauerkraut, and kimchi contain probiotics—live cultures that amplify good bacteria.

Stay well hydrated to support regular bowel movements and limit consumption of highly processed foods. Artificial sweeteners, emulsifiers, and other food additives can harm microbial populations. Reduce stress through yoga, meditation, nature walks, or other relaxing activities. Get at least 7 hours of quality sleep a night.

Strategic use of gut-health **supplements** can also help nurture microbiome balance. Prebiotic supplements provide soluble fiber, which fuels microbiome growth. Common prebiotics include inulin, fructooligosaccharides (FOS), and galactooligosaccharides. Probiotic supplements deliver specific strains linked to weight management, like Lactobacillus gasseri, Lactobacillus rhamnosus, and Bifidobacterium lactis.

Consider getting your microbiome tested to obtain personalized recommendations. Based on your unique gut profile, nutritional therapists can suggest targeted prebiotics, probiotics, and postbiotics to correct dysbiosis. Postbiotics are bacterial byproducts that convey health benefits.

Implementing a comprehensive gut health plan enhances metabolic flexibility and fat-burning capacity by optimizing microbiome balance and function. Feed your good gut bacteria through smart dietary choices and supplements. Reduce microbiome-disrupting habits. Remember, your gut health strongly influences your ability to maintain an ideal weight and metabolism.

The Impact of Environmental Factors

The environments we live, work, and play in have a significant impact on our metabolic health. Factors such as air quality, access to nature, noise pollution, and weather patterns have an impact on physiology and behavior in ways that affect weight management and metabolism. As our surroundings become more artificial and disconnected from nature, we disregard how the environment molds our health. Adjusting certain environmental variables can enhance or impair your body's innate fat-burning mechanisms.

Perhaps the most apparent link is between **air pollution** and metabolic disease. Air pollutants like particulate matter, nitrogen oxides, sulfur oxides, and heavy metals trigger systemic inflammation and oxidative stress. This impairs glucose and lipid metabolism, spurring insulin resistance and a higher risk of obesity, diabetes, and cardiovascular disease. Even short-term exposure to traffic exhaust fumes can reduce insulin sensitivity and blood vessel function. Seek out clean-air environments as much as possible. Use high-quality air filters at home and wear an appropriate mask during activities like commuting or exercising outdoors in heavy smog.

Lack of exposure to natural environments also correlates to poorer metabolic health. Bright **sunlight** helps regulate circadian biology and vitamin D synthesis, both of which influence weight control and inflammation. The microbes and phytoncides released by plants impart benefits we've not fully grasped. Spending time outside hiking, gardening, or just being surrounded by greenery also provides a measure of stress relief. Urbanization and inadequate environmental exposure hamper metabolic functioning.

Noise pollution is another concern. Chronic loud noise from airports, construction, or crowded city streets elevates stress hormones and blood pressure, promoting insulin resistance. Finding pockets of quietude through noise-blocking headphones, meditation, or time in nature helps offset these adverse effects.

Even something as simple as **room temperature** matters. Studies show ambient temperatures around 66°F enhance brown fat activity and insulin sensitivity compared to warmer conditions. Avoid very chilled indoor environments as well, as this requires the body to work harder to maintain core temperature.

Optimizing environmental factors bolsters metabolic health and weight control in research-backed ways. While we can't control all aspects of our surroundings, being mindful of modifications that reduce pollution exposure, increase nature interactions, minimize noise, and stabilize comfortable room temperatures can help sustain metabolic balance. External variables impact our physiology to a greater extent than we may realize. Fine-tuning your environment removes certain impediments to a healthy metabolism.

Creating a Supportive Environment

Succeeding with any diet or fitness program requires having a supportive environment. Your home, workplace, and social circles can either bolster your metabolic health efforts or derail them. It's essential to curate surroundings that empower you to make positive choices. This enhances self-efficacy and long-term sustainability.

- Start by assessing your **home environment**. Remove tempting junk foods and beverages. Stock your kitchen with healthy ingredients and batch-cook meals for the week ahead. Prepare balanced snacks like nuts, fruits, and veggies to grab easily when hunger strikes. Display motivational notes and progress photos where you'll see them. Declutter to reduce stress.
- **Structure your home** to facilitate activity. Walking even short distances accumulates extra calories. Take calls on the go and march in place during commercials. Place exercise equipment in front of the TV. Schedule activity breaks on your calendar. The more movement woven into your home routine, the better.
- Inform your **family** and roommates about your program, and enlist their assistance. Request help with healthy food prep or home-cooked meals. Plan active outings together. Ask them not to bring trigger foods home or to indulge away from you. Mutual accountability helps.
- Likewise, talk to **coworkers** about your goals. Ask them to refrain from bringing in candy or baked goods as gifts. Bring your own lunch and snacks so you stay in control. Add healthy dishes to office potlucks. To break up sedentary time, walk laps or use the stairs in the morning and mid-afternoon. Stay hydrated with a water bottle handy.
- Avoid **office treats**, **happy hours**, and other indulgences. With humor, politely turn down food pushers or peer pressure. Frame it positively: "No thanks, I'm watching my health." Share your journey to inspire others, too. Enlist workout buddies for added motivation.
- Manage **social occasions** judiciously. Suggest active meetups, such as hikes or sports, over food-centric ones. Contribute a healthy dish to gatherings. Focus conversations on positive topics rather than complaints. Limit alcohol. Surround yourself with supportive, like-minded people when possible. Don't feel pressured to overeat or drink.
- Retail settings can also derail progress with tempting aromas and signs that encourage impulse buys. Opt for shorter **shopping trips** during off-peak hours when stores are less chaotic. Shop perimeter aisles where healthier whole foods predominate. Avoid idling too long in the bakery or snack aisles. Make lists and stick to them.

Creating an environment with cues and habits that reinforce your metabolic health goals requires forethought, but it pays off enormously. You gain constant subconscious nudges to make sound choices that enhance your diet, activity, and mindset. With supportive surroundings, you're better able to maintain the lifestyle factors that drive sustainable weight-loss success.

CHAPTER 8: IMPLEMENTING METABOLIC CONFUSION

Setting Realistic Goals

The path to reaching your health and fitness objectives begins with defining realistic goals. Many embark on their journey with unrealistic expectations that set them up for frustration and failure. Creating achievable goals requires self-reflection, planning, and commitment.

1. When establishing your goals, first take an honest look at where you currently stand in terms of your health, fitness level, schedule, and other lifestyle factors. Understanding your **starting point** gives a baseline for mapping meaningful progress. Those new to improving their health may need to begin slowly with foundational changes before taking on more ambitious goals. Be aware of any physical limitations or injuries that necessitate changing certain activities.

2. Next, articulate your **motivation** and **priorities**. Losing weight quickly may be less sustainable than building lifelong healthy habits. Your reasons for wanting change will impact the goals you choose. List your "why" statements, like improving energy, feeling confident, reducing disease risk, or keeping up with kids. Revisit these motivators whenever you need inspiration.

3. Now break down big-picture goals into smaller, **incremental steps**. Plan targets for the next 1-3 months, 6 months, year, and beyond. Having both short- and long-term goals helps you tackle large objectives by taking them one day at a time. Progress happens through small, repeated actions compounded over time.

4. Ensure your goals reflect the **SMART framework**: specific, measurable, achievable, relevant, and time-bound. Clearly define what you will achieve and by what time. "Lose weight" is vague, but "lose 10 pounds in 3 months" is specific. Make goals quantifiable so you can track advancement. Select objectives within your capacity, given other commitments. The relevance ties back to your underlying motivations.

5. When gauging achievability, consider your current fitness level, nutrition habits, schedule, responsibilities, and any limitations requiring **accommodation**. Be honest about any obstacles that may impede your goals. For example, nursing an injury may require modifying certain exercises. Building in flexibility helps anticipate potential setbacks.

6. Goals centered on **behaviors within your control** rather than outcomes are often more effective. Focus on actions like strength training three times per week, limiting processed foods, and walking 30 minutes daily. The results will naturally follow as you stick to beneficial habits over time. Celebrate small wins along the way.

7. To stay on track, **write down** your SMART goals somewhere visible to serve as a constant reminder. Share your plans with supportive friends and family to build accountability. Set goals for your calendar and daily routine. Anticipate busy periods that may derail progress and develop contingency plans.

8. **Monitor advancements** weekly and monthly. Reflect on what is going well and make any necessary changes. Be prepared to adapt your goals based on life changes and new capabilities gained. Expect setbacks and plateaus—persist through them by modifying your approach rather than abandoning goals altogether.

9. **Patience** and **compassion** for yourself throughout the process are vital. Progress often unfolds gradually, with ups and downs along the way. Avoid extreme or unsustainable practices that are unlikely to last. Make your plan enjoyable by using activities you like. The journey should enhance life's pleasures rather than restrict them.

10. Surround yourself with **positive influences**, leading by example. Seek resources, tools, or professional guidance as needed. However, realize that you are ultimately responsible for the commitment and work required to accomplish your goals.

Setting SMART goals rooted in your values and taking incremental steps put you on the path to meaningful change. Allow the process to build confidence, resilience, and new capabilities. Focus on consistency more than perfection. With realistic goals and dedication, you can gain the health, fitness, and fulfillment you desire. The journey requires patience, adaptability, and belief in yourself. Take it one day and make one positive choice at a time, moving forward. You've got this!

Preparing Mentally and Physically

Embarking on a fitness and nutrition journey requires preparation on both a mental and physical level. Without adequate groundwork, attempts at change often fizzle out when motivation wanes or challenges arise.

On the mental front, be clear on why you want to make certain changes. **Solid reasons** beyond vanity, like improving your health or keeping up with kids, provide intrinsic motivation that helps weather setbacks. Envision your ideal future self and how you'll feel after achieving your goals. This provides a purpose during difficult times.

1. Set **SMART goals** with tangible **steps** to create a defined map. Without plans, vague resolutions quickly fall apart. Break larger goals down into smaller milestones that are celebrated along the way. Share your intentions with supportive people to build accountability.
2. Address any **limiting beliefs** that could sabotage you. "I don't have enough willpower" becomes a self-fulfilling prophecy. Challenge negative thought patterns and build self-efficacy by highlighting past successes. You have accomplished hard things before.
3. Strengthen **resilience** for when plans go awry. Perfection is unsustainable. Anticipate challenges such as illness, injury, or busy periods. Have contingency plans to get quickly back on track rather than abandoning the ship. Reframe setbacks as opportunities for improvement.
4. Stock up on **motivational resources**. Inspiring podcasts, audiobooks, and printed quotes reinforce why you're undertaking this journey. Refer to these when you need a boost. Surround yourself with positive influences, leading by example.
5. On the physical side, consult your **doctor**, especially if you have existing medical issues. Get baseline metrics like weight, body fat percentage, and bloodwork. Address any nutrient deficiencies, metabolic conditions, or injuries needing rehabilitation.
6. Start slowly and **progress gradually** to avoid burnout and minimize injury risk. Attempting too much too fast often backfires. Build a fitness base before advancing. Allow time for your body to adapt to new demands.
7. Incorporate **active recovery** like stretching, foam rolling, massage, and sleep. This allows your body to recharge and actually get fitter during rest periods. Schedule adequate downtime between intense training sessions.
8. Dial in your nutrition foundation before implementing advanced techniques like intermittent fasting or carb cycling. First, work on the **basics**, such as hitting macro targets, hydration, nutrition timing, and including enough vegetables.
9. **Experiment** with different forms of movement and foods you enjoy. Tailor activities and meals to fit your preferences and lifestyle. Adopting major dislikes won't last. Selecting nutritious foods you genuinely enjoy makes healthy eating sustainable.

10. Clean out your **pantry** and **fridge**. Stock up on items that align with your program, like produce, lean proteins, healthy fats, and nutritious snacks. Meal prep elements like batch-cooked grains and prepped veggies for easy assembly.

11. Reduce **temptations**, especially at the start when willpower is vulnerable. Don't keep trigger foods at home, relying on willpower alone. Make the healthy option the easy default.

12. Prepare food and gym bags **in advance**. When out and about, pack snacks with healthy options. Eliminate unnecessary decisions that can derail your plan. During busy times, run on autopilot.

13. Tell **friends** and **family** about your new regimen to curb social pressures. Suggest active social outings, such as hiking or cooking healthy meals together. Enlist an "accountability buddy" to check in on your progress.

14. Address any **equipment** needs before beginning, like kitchen tools, a fitness tracker, or a gym membership. Gathering key items eliminates future excuses and delays.

15. Make fitness a part of your **identity**, not just something you do periodically. Say "I am an athlete" or "I am a healthy eater" rather than "I am trying to exercise more" or "I am dieting." Your mindset matters.

16. **Schedule** workouts and meal prep like any other important appointment. Block time on your calendar and set reminders. Consistency is key, even on busy days. Prepare for travel or holidays to stay on course.

When ramping up your fitness and nutrition program, you can hit the ground running by laying mental and physical groundwork. Anticipate obstacles, build resilience, curate your environment, and embark gradually. Establishing a solid foundation enables you to persist and prosper in the long run.

Weekly and Monthly Planning

Achieving fitness and nutrition goals requires diligent planning on a weekly and monthly basis. Failing to plan means planning to fail. Dedicate time to intentionally map out workouts, meals, and other key elements that support your overall objectives. Think through how each day and week will realistically unfold.

1. Start by reviewing your overarching **goals** and milestone targets. This provides focus and motivation as you construct your plan. Identify upcoming events or schedule changes needing accommodation, like vacations, busy work periods, or holidays.

2. Build your **weekly** plan backward, starting with fixed items first, like workout classes or regular appointments. Schedule exercise each week first, as this is foundational. Dedicate the time like any other non-negotiable commitment. Ensure you include adequate recovery built in, such as 1-2 rest days and post-workout mobility work.

3. Next, plug in **meal planning** and prep sessions. This includes grocery shopping, batch cooking, washing produce, pre-portioning snacks, etc. Schedule these routinely, like you would recurring meetings. Prepare for busy days by preparing ingredients or meals in advance.

4. Pepper can incorporate additional **health-promoting practices** such as meditation, visualization, journaling, or learning a new relevant skill. Weave these into the calendar to prevent neglecting the mental side. This cultivates the identity and mindset to stick with your plan.

5. Within your exercise and nutrition schedule, overlay **variation** into the plan to continually progress and prevent plateaus. This includes alternating strength training focus (upper vs.

lower body), cardio modes (running vs. cycling), weekly workout layout, rep ranges, macro cycles, and calories.

6. Look for potential bottlenecks where overlapping commitments could compromise your regimen. Identify areas where you will need contingency plans, such as getting up early, preparing grab-and-go meals, or condensing workouts. Life happens; **anticipate obstacles**.

7. Schedule **relaxation** and social time to avoid burnout. All work and no play is unsustainable. Include fun activities, time with friends and family, and rest. Protect your sleep schedule, especially on hard training days.

8. Assign **specific tasks** to be completed each day in accordance with your program. Having defined action steps makes execution more automatic versus vague aspirations. Break bigger goals into tangible, bite-sized next steps to maintain momentum.

9. At the close of each week, do a **review**. Assess what went well and where you need to improve for the upcoming week. Reflect on patterns or problem areas that require adjustment. Revisit and update your plan on a weekly basis.

10. From your weekly plans, develop your **monthly** outlook. This provides a higher-level view, allowing you to build progression, adequate recovery, and needed variety into your program month-to-month. You can also prepare for larger upcoming events.

11. Look at the monthly training load and distribution of harder vs. easier days. Avoid packing too many heavy training blocks together without breaks. Periodize your training month-to-month to peak for key events, then recover.

12. Layer in **new** challenges, workouts, skills, or nutrition approaches each month to keep your body adapting rather than hitting a plateau. To avoid overdoing it, strategically introduce these at a sustainable rate.

13. Use your monthly view to see **bigger lifestyle patterns** that may be hindering you, like frequent work travel or social engagements derailing your regimen. Identify these early and develop solutions.

14. **Revisit** your monthly plan weekly. Make any needed adjustments based on your weekly check-ins, energy levels, and life circumstances. Planning is a dynamic process, not a static .

The combination of intentional weekly and monthly plans will bolster your chances of realizing your fitness and nutrition goals. Dedicate time to map these out thoroughly and revisit them on a regular basis. Effective planning translates aspirations into consistent action.

Tracking Your Progress

Monitoring your advancement is essential for achieving fitness and nutrition goals. What gets measured gets managed. Tracking key metrics makes your progress tangible and exposes what's working versus needing adjustment.

1. Begin by establishing **baseline measurements** before starting your program. Weight, body composition, cardiovascular endurance, strength levels, bloodwork, circumference measurements, and progress photos provide comparison points.

2. Define what **metrics** align with your specific goals to track consistently. If you are aiming for weight loss, measure your weight and waist circumference. If you're looking for strength gains, try maximal lifts. Ensure your tracked metrics genuinely reflect progress rather than extraneous fluctuations.

3. Determine the optimal tracking **frequency** for each metric based on your goals. Weight can be measured daily or weekly, bloodwork every few months, and progress photos taken monthly. Avoid overtesting metrics that change slowly or cause anxiety.

4. For accurate comparisons, be **consistent** with tracking conditions. After using the bathroom, weigh first thing in the morning. Each time, take progress photos in the same lighting and poses. Use the same equipment and testing protocol.

5. **Record** all metrics in one place, like a journal, online document, or app. This helps detect patterns over time. Include notes on factors that may influence results, like sleep, stress, diet changes, etc. Reference this log to identify what's working.

6. Beyond objective data, track **subjective markers** like energy, cravings, hunger levels, mood, digestion, appetite, and workout recovery. These provide insight into how your program is functioning.

7. **Celebrate** small wins and milestones met along the way, like strength gains, inches lost, hitting macro targets, establishing new habits, improved lab results, etc. Recognize advancement beyond just the number on the scale.

8. Learn your unique **body signals** indicating proper training, nutrition, and recovery. Include factors such as soreness levels, menstrual cycle phases, hunger cues, and sleep quality in your regimen.

9. As needed, **adjust** your tracking metrics and frequency based on emerging goals and individual responses. For example, increasing protein intake if strength gains plateau or reducing training volume if chronically fatigued.

10. Beware of putting **too much** stock in day-to-day fluctuations. To assess true progress, look at overall trends over several weeks and months. Be patient; meaningful change takes time and consistency.

11. Avoid **emotional** attachment to tracking metrics and numbers that cross certain thresholds. Progress is not linear. Expect setbacks and course corrections using tracking insights.

12. Use **technology** like wearables, apps, and spreadsheets to simplify data gathering, aggregation, and analysis. However, do not become overly reliant on technology. Listen to your body's innate signals too.

13. **Share** tracking data with your support team, like a coach, doctor, dietician, or knowledgeable friend, for further input. But beware of comparisons with others' stats. Focus on your personal progression.

14. Remain **flexible** and **open** to modifying your plan based on tracked results and emerging challenges. Expect to make adjustments over time as your needs change. Be responsive, not rigid.

15. **Balance** diligent tracking with avoiding obsession. Do not compulsively over-measure or become consumed with the numbers. Keep perspective on your larger health goals.

16. Pat yourself on the back for adhering to **consistent** tracking itself, regardless of the recorded metrics. Tracking is a success, reflecting your dedication and follow-through.

By regularly monitoring your progress using key metrics, you gain insight into what propels you towards your fitness and nutrition goals. Tracking enhances clarity, motivation, troubleshooting, and the customization of your plan. Stay consistent, responsive, and balanced. The numbers do not define you. Consistency in the process matters most on your unique journey. Keep perspective. Progress takes patience and imperfection. You've got this!

Adjusting Your Plan as Needed

An effective fitness and nutrition plan must be a living document that evolves over time. Rigidly adhering to a static plan is a recipe for frustration and failure. As your body and life circumstances change, you must be prepared to fluidly adapt.

1. Begin with the mentality that program adjustments are not only expected but also **required** for sustained success. Progress is rarely linear. Accept that ups and downs are normal, even when diligently executing. Be flexible rather than fixated on following a plan perfectly.
2. Remain attentive to your **mind** and **body's signals**, indicating when it may be time for modifications. Symptoms like plateaus, chronic fatigue, irritability, cravings, insomnia, and hormonal changes all warrant checking in on potential adjustments needed.
3. Use **objective** tracking data like strength gains, weight loss, body measurements, and bloodwork to reveal when your current approach is no longer working optimally. Let the numbers guide evidence-based change.
4. **Reevaluate** your regimen following major life changes like a new job, relationship, relocated residence, pregnancy, or injury. Your program must fit your current lifestyle and physical status.
5. After an illness, injury, or extended break, **ease back** into training progressively. Temporarily reduce volume, intensity, and duration until you rebuild your base. A slower ramp-up helps prevent setbacks.
6. As your fitness improves, incrementally **increase challenges** such as heavier weights, higher intensity intervals, new exercises, and reduced rest periods. Stagnation necessitates a stimulus change.
7. **Variate** your **nutrition** plan through calorie cycling, macro manipulation, meal timing shifts, new cuisine, supplement use, intermittent fasting, and ketogenic periods. Maintain your body's metabolic flexibility.
8. Counteract **stressors** by adjusting **recovery** practices like meditation, massage, mobility work, and sleep habits. Allow time to restore mental and physical balance.
9. Conduct periodic **progress check-ins**, such as every 1-3 months, assessing what to maintain versus modify moving forward based on your goals and current state.
10. During **periods** of demanding travel, reduced sleep, or intense stress, temporarily **dial back** your regimen by reducing volume, intensity, and overall demands to avoid overtraining.
11. If you feel burned out mentally or physically, take a planned **break** from rigid structures. Enjoy some time exploring different activities and less-tracked nutrition approaches. Recharge your motivation.
12. Periodically, **collaborate** with a coach or knowledgeable professional to inspect your plan with fresh eyes. They may identify needed modifications that you overlook while deep in the weeds.
13. Remain philosophically **open-minded** and willing to explore new modalities and philosophies. Rigidly adhering to one approach limits your growth. Expose yourself to fresh perspectives.
14. **Trust** that, with consistent effort, active adjustments, and patience, you will navigate valleys and plateaus over time. Progress ebbs and flows. Persistence through shifts will pay off.

By embracing flexibility and actively modifying components when needed, you enable your fitness regimen to stand the test of time. Treat your plan as a dynamic framework to evolve rather than a static doctrine. Adjust intelligently and stay on course. Consistency with prudent change will drive results as you continually progress along your journey. You've got this!

CHAPTER 9: TROUBLESHOOTING COMMON CHALLENGES

Overcoming Plateaus

Hitting a plateau while trying to lose weight can be incredibly frustrating. You've been diligently following your diet and exercise plan, yet the scale refuses to budge. Rest assured, this is a common challenge faced by many on their weight-loss journey. With some targeted strategies, you can break through this plateau and get back on track with your goals.

- The first key is identifying the potential **causes** of your plateau. There are a few main culprits that could be sabotaging your progress. First, you may have hit a point where your body has adapted to your current calorie intake and workout regimen. When you diet, your metabolism can slow down as your body aims to conserve energy. Similarly, doing the same exercises week after week can lead to a plateau as your muscles become more efficient at that specific routine.

- The solution is to incorporate more **variety** to throw your body off balance and reboot your results. This metabolic confusion technique challenges your body in new ways with dietary changes and varied training. Strategically cycling your calories or alternating between higher and lower-calorie days is one approach. This helps prevent your metabolism from downshifting to match a consistent calorie deficit. Manipulating your carb intake through carb cycling is another option, capitalizing on how carbs influence fat-burning hormones. You can also build in a couple refeed days where you increase calories from carbs to boost leptin levels.

- On the fitness side, **cross-training** is key to overcoming an exercise plateau. Replace some of your regular cardio with HIIT sessions, take a dance or spin class, or try new equipment like a rowing machine or kettlebells. Weightlifters should change up their main lifts, rep ranges, and volume. Add in new exercises that work the muscles from different angles. Keeping your body guessing will consistently lead to results. Just be sure not to overdo new, intense workouts to avoid injury or burnout.

- Sometimes a plateau happens simply because your **calorie intake** has creeped up without you realizing it. Track your food intake for a week to identify any extra servings, oils, condiments, or cheat meals that have added hidden calories. These little extras can quickly erase your deficit. Similarly, you may be underestimating your portion sizes or calorie counts. Weighing food rather than eyeballing servings will allow for more accurate tracking. Be vigilant about tracking every bite—those handfuls of nuts or tastes while cooking all count. If needed, trim about 100–200 calories per day to create a clearer deficit.

- Along with calories, reassess your **macro targets**. Make sure your protein intake is sufficient to spare muscle mass when in a caloric deficit; shoot for 0.7–1 gram per pound of body weight daily. Fill the rest of your calories with nutrient-dense complex carbs and healthy fats. Limit your intake of processed carbs and sugary treats as they provide empty calories. Prioritize whole foods that offer more vitamins, minerals, and fiber.

- After weeks or months of dieting, you may need to take a short **diet break** to reset. This could be 1-2 weeks at maintenance calories, allowing your body to rebalance hormones like leptin and thyroid that influence weight loss. You don't want to lose momentum with too long of a break, though. Use this time to recharge motivation and fine-tune your plan of attack for enhanced results when you restart your deficit.

- Managing **stress** is another factor, as high cortisol can stall fat loss. Build in more rest days if you've been overtraining. Make sleep a priority, aiming for 7-9 hours per night. Practice relaxation techniques such as meditation, yoga, deep breathing, or massage therapy to decompress. Evaluate other potential stress triggers and tackle any issues head-on.

- **Patience** and **consistency** will be required to push through this plateau period. Trust in your program, and avoid extreme measures like excessively slashing calories or overdoing cardio. Stick with the process, continuing to progress, and challenging yourself over time. With some tenacity, the weight will begin to drop again. Consistently fueling your body well and working those muscles hard is a recipe for success.

If you still find the scale unmoving after 4-6 weeks of earnest effort adjusting these variables, consult a professional. A registered dietitian can assess your diet and pinpoint trouble areas. Discussing a customized nutrition or training plan could provide new insights into progress. With some determination and targeted tweaks, the plateau will pass. You'll be back on your way toward crushing those weight-loss goals.

Dealing with Cravings

Cravings can feel like an irresistible force when you're trying to lose weight. The sight or smell of an indulgent food can instantly trigger an intense desire that hijacks your healthy eating goals. However, with the right strategies, you can beat those pesky cravings and stay on track.

- First, it helps to **understand** what is happening **biologically** when a craving strikes. The limbic system in the brain plays a key role, triggering the release of dopamine and opioids that make you anticipate reward from giving in to the craving. Ghrelin, the "hunger hormone," surges, while leptin, which signals satiety, drops. These hormonal shifts boost appetite. Blood sugar dips can also spark cravings for a quick carb fix.
- Knowing what's behind the urge makes it easier to take control. One approach is to **distract** yourself from the craving. Go for a walk, call a friend, immerse yourself in a hobby, or engage in any activity that breaks the mental fixation. Setting a timer for 15 minutes can help you ride out an intense wave of hunger until it passes. Visualization is another technique for picturing how you'll feel if you give in vs. if you succeed in moving past the urge.
- **Planning** is essential to preventing cravings from striking in the first place. Make sure you're eating enough protein, fiber, and healthy fats to sustain energy and fullness between meals. Schedule snacks to prevent blood sugar dips, and prepare healthy options you enjoy to grab quickly when needed. Stay hydrated, since thirst signals can disguise themselves as hunger.
- **Prepare** for challenging scenarios to get ahead of situational cravings. Have a protein bar with you when running errands past bakeries or ice cream shops. Before attending social events where indulgent party foods may tempt you, eat a healthy meal. Identify triggers that spark specific cravings, like late-night snacking while watching TV, then set up guardrails like avoiding screens after 9 p.m. or limiting snacks to cut veggies and hummus.
- When a craving does arise, one simple option is to **delay** acting on it. Tell yourself that you can indulge later if the craving persists, and keep postponing to push past the initial intensity until it passes. Having a healthy substitute can also help satisfy the urge with less harm, like fresh fruit if sweets are calling your name.
- If **emotional eating** is fueling cravings, get to the root cause. Exercise, social connection, relaxing hobbies, or therapies like meditation can all naturally boost mood. Manage stress with better work-life balance, delegating responsibilities, or setting more realistic expectations. Identify negative thought patterns triggering emotional overeating, then reframe these with positive self-talk. Professional counseling can also help develop coping mechanisms beyond food.

- Pay attention to inadequate body fueling as well, which can lead to rebound hunger and cravings. Ensure your diet has the right **balance** of **macronutrients**: lean protein, fiber-rich complex carbs, and healthy fats. Front-load calories earlier in the day, when activity is highest. Stay hydrated between meals. Pay attention to your body's internal signals of hunger and fullness to distinguish between a genuine need for more food and a mere craving.
- **Supplements** like glucomannan fiber, chromium picolinate, and alpha-lipoic acid can aid with blood sugar management and appetite control. Caffeine may help curb cravings in the in the short term but cause hunger to rebound later on. Carefully weigh the risks and benefits before using diet pills, which carry side effects.
- The most powerful craving crusher is being mentally **prepared** to navigate the inevitable challenges that will arise in any weight-loss journey. Have go-to techniques established. Visualize success beforehand. Cultivate self-discipline while also practicing self-compassion if perfection is unrealistic. Remind yourself regularly why your health and body goals matter to reinforce motivation when it wavers.

You can always overcome sporadic cravings with diligence and commitment to the process. Staying focused on the big picture will help short-term urges lose their power over you. Each small victory in resisting temptation builds confidence and new habits. You can gain control over those cravings and continue moving forward on your weight-loss path. Consistency is key, along with having tools ready to deploy in moments of vulnerability. With perseverance and the right mindset, cravings will become less frequent and easier to handle over time. Stick with it until healthy eating patterns are firmly embedded in your new normal.

Managing Social Situations

Social events can be a diet danger zone when you're trying to lose weight. Parties, restaurants, holidays, and get-togethers often center around tempting foods that derail healthy eating.

- First, go into any social situation with an **eating game plan**. Take a look at the menu or party spread in advance, if possible, and decide what fits into your diet. Lean proteins, veggies, and lighter apps are always solid choices. Load up on the crudité platter. Ask about prep methods; grilled, steamed, or roasted are better than fried. Don't arrive starving, which clouds judgment; have a healthy snack beforehand.
- When mingling, hold a low-calorie **drink** like seltzer to keep hands busy. To avoid mindless grazing, first position yourself across the room from the food. Scope out all the options before taking a plate. Use smaller plates, which psychologically prompt modest portions. Fill half your plate with salad or vegetables first, then add reasonable amounts of proteins and smart starches like brown rice or quinoa.
- If indulging in a **special occasion** treat, sustainably fit it into your calorie budget. Compensate by eating lighter the rest of the day or exercising more. Enjoy a true favorite food mindfully—savor each bite rather than devouring it thoughtlessly. Share a dessert with friends. Bring a nutritious dish that you can fill up on.
- To manage **alcohol** calories, alternate drinks with water or seltzer. Opt for wine or champagne over sugary cocktails or beer. Hold the extras like sugary mixers. For daytime gatherings, stick with low-cal options like iced tea, black coffee, or mineral water.
- Polite **refusal skills** will also serve you well. Turn down plates or offers for second helpings by thanking the host, but note that you are satisfied. To shift the focus from food, suggest catching up over an activity rather than meals. You can always take leftovers home if something looks too delicious to resist.

- For challenges like **happy hours**, order a salad with protein or a veggie-based appetizer. Satisfy snack cravings with fresh salsa and guacamole instead of baskets of fried bar food. Avoid mindless munching on bowls of nuts or chips on the table. Manage alcohol intake and stay alert to prevent lowered inhibitions leading to poor choices.
- Establish **yourself** as someone who enjoys a balance of healthy and indulgent foods. Share your newest go-to recipe so friends see your diet isn't about deprivation. Avoid labeling foods as "good" or "bad," which sets up guilt complexes; instead, focus on how certain choices make you feel energized or sluggish. Lead by example by trying new nutritious dishes.
- Stay **motivated** by focusing on how being healthy and active allows you to more fully engage with loved ones. Set an intention before each event to make choices that serve your goals. Chat with a supportive friend in attendance who can be an accountability partner. Make sure to adhere to your plan to the best of your ability, and then promptly resume your progress.

With preparation and purpose, social situations don't have to upend your progress. Clear strategies give you confidence to navigate inevitable temptations without an internal tug-of-war. The more consistently you make smart choices that align with your health goals, the easier it becomes over time. Prioritize how you want to feel—lighter and more energetic, or overindulged and lethargic. Staying on course leads to more fun and long-term enjoyment of social gatherings without guilt. You've got this!

Adjusting to Life Changes

Life is full of changes that can shake up your weight loss efforts, from new jobs to moves to relationships evolving. Major adjustments often disrupt normal routines and introduce new sources of stress that sabotage healthy habits. With some thoughtful planning, you can adapt to maintain momentum even when circumstances are in flux.

- Start by identifying any upcoming transitions that could throw you off course. **Anticipating** challenges is the first step to circumventing them. If you're moving, research gyms, grocery options, and dining spots near your new home to ensure you'll have access to support your program. Stock up on staple foods to ease the initial transition. Plan to batch cook and meal prep first thing in your new kitchen to set yourself up for controlled eating while adjusting to new surroundings.
- When beginning a **new job**, set your alarm to allow time for exercise before work if that has been your routine. Find out if the office has a gym or showers to facilitate working out over a lunch break. Scope out healthy eating options nearby so you have go-to spots identified. Pack lunch to avoid the tempting spreads frequently found in company cafeterias. Schedule reminders to stay hydrated since it's easy to forget when engrossed in new tasks.
- Any significant change necessitates intensifying organization and preparation to prevent unpreparedness during vulnerable times. Carve out time on weekends to **plan weekly menus** and get groceries. Add workout sessions to your calendar and prioritize them amidst other demands. Set reminders to stay on top of behaviors that tend to slip, like water consumption or logging food. Having structured routines and habits in place creates stability during turbulent times.
- Staying connected to your **support system** is also essential when going through adjustments. Reach out to loved ones, a trainer, or colleagues you've bonded with over healthy lifestyles. Share that you may need extra accountability as you navigate changes. Having a motivational partner makes it easier to decline happy hour drinks after a stressful workday or get up for an early run when exhausted from moving boxes. Use technology such as fitness trackers and food logging apps to maintain your accountability.

- **Adaptability** is critical when inevitable curveballs arise. Expect setbacks and make contingency plans. If stuck working late, keep a backup meal in the fridge to heat up rather than resorting to takeout. Have frozen smoothies or a protein bar if the disrupted morning makes a workout impossible. Build in off-ramps when traveling, like researching gyms to drop-in on or packing resistant bands to keep up some exercise. Adjust your mindset as well; perfection is unrealistic amidst changes, but staying committed to consistency is key.
- Look at **transitional periods** as opportunities to develop new healthy habits and behaviors. Experiment with new recipes, fitness classes, or walking paths near your new home. Make a fresh start nutritionally by overhauling your pantry and meal planning. Disruption brings the chance to create better routines. Make self-care and stress management even more of a priority during hectic times.
- Finally, be **patient** with yourself and acknowledge that adjustment takes time. Expect some missteps as you establish new rhythms and patterns. Refocus on the big picture; a few indulgent meals or missed workouts in the short term won't derail you. With preparation and resilience, you'll navigate bumps on the road back to making consistent progress. Keep your end goal in sight and trust that staying on course will get you there, even if the path looks different than expected. You've got this!

When to Seek Professional Help

Embarking on a weight loss journey on your own takes dedication, but there are times when it can be invaluable to seek outside expertise. The right professionals can provide tailored guidance, support, and accountability to help you overcome obstacles. Knowing when to reach out can mean the difference between continued frustration and renewed progress.

- Working with a registered **dietitian** is advisable if you need help constructing a customized nutrition plan based on your health profile, lifestyle factors, and body goals. They can run diagnostic testing to pinpoint any underlying issues, advise on your ideal macronutrient balance and caloric needs, and ensure you are fueling your body safely and adequately while in a deficit. Ongoing counseling provides accountability as well, so you stick to the plan.
- If **emotional** or binge eating is derailing your efforts, seeking help from an **eating disorder** specialist, **psychologist**, or psychiatrist can be beneficial. They will work to uncover the root causes driving these behaviors, equip you with coping strategies beyond food to manage stressors and emotions, and shift your mindset toward a healthier relationship with food. People often use cognitive behavioral therapy to alter deeply ingrained thought patterns.
- If you suspect your plateau or weight gain could be tied to **hormonal** imbalances, see an **endocrinologist**. They can test for potential issues with thyroid, cortisol, insulin resistance, or reproductive hormones that make weight loss difficult. Medication or supplements may help correct the imbalance, in combination with dietary changes. Those with PCOS often find low-carb diets effective, for example.
- A **personal trainer** is advisable if you need guidance designing an exercise program to complement your diet efforts. They can assess your fitness level, limitations, and goals, then structure a plan specific to your needs. You'll perform exercises with proper form to avoid injury. Sessions provide accountability, while their encouragement pushes you past mental blocks. If cost is a barrier, consider small-group training.
- For musculoskeletal injuries, a **physical therapist** can provide rehabilitation exercises and treatment to help you resume activity as soon as you are safely able. They also identify any biomechanical issues or postural dysfunctions that may be exacerbating discomfort and then provide corrective strategies. Consulting an orthopedic specialist is wise if injury symptoms

do not improve within 1-2 months with conservative care. In some cases, surgery might be necessary.

- If you believe **medications** could be impacting your weight, discuss options with the prescribing **doctor**. Adjusting dosage or trialing alternatives may offer relief from side effects like fluid retention, constant hunger, or fatigue, which create obstacles. Make sure they are monitoring indicators like blood pressure and glucose to ensure your health doesn't decline amidst medication changes.
- A **life coach** specializing in health and wellness can help if you need assistance building more structure and productive **habits**. They keep you accountable to goals, identify self-sabotaging thoughts and behaviors that require reframing, and provide motivation during those times when your own reserves are running low. Coaches equip you with the skills to prioritize self-care amidst life's demands.

Knowing when to seek help takes honesty about what is and isn't currently working. Continual frustration, struggle with the same hurdles, emotional exhaustion, loss of motivation, or health concerns are all signs it may be time to consider outside support. The right guidance can provide a reset when you've lost your way. Taking this step is courageous, not a defeat.

At the same time, remember that lifestyle change requires personal ownership in the end. No professional can do the hard day-to-day work for you. Collaborate with them to map out a plan, then get ready to put it into consistent action. Approach the process with humility, patience, and openness to make the most of their guidance. With an expert support team behind you, breakthroughs will happen.

CHAPTER 10: BEYOND WEIGHT LOSS: LONG-TERM HEALTH BENEFITS

Improved Cardiovascular Health

A healthy heart and cardiovascular system are key to overall health and longevity. When it comes to weight loss, improving cardiovascular health provides benefits that go far beyond just losing pounds. Implementing a comprehensive metabolic confusion program that incorporates strategic exercise, nutrition, and lifestyle components can profoundly impact heart health in numerous ways.

First and foremost, **losing** excess **body fat** reduces strain on the heart. Obesity forces the heart to pump harder to supply blood to all that extra tissue. Just a 10% reduction in body weight can lower bad LDL cholesterol, triglycerides, and blood pressure while increasing good HDL cholesterol. This directly improves cardiovascular risk factors. Losing weight can also help reduce inflammation in the body, which further alleviates pressure on the heart.

Adopting **healthy eating habits** full of whole, unprocessed foods like fruits, vegetables, lean proteins, whole grains, nuts, and seeds provides antioxidants, fiber, and important micronutrients. These nutrients reduce systemic inflammation, cholesterol levels, and plaque buildup in the arteries. In particular, eating foods high in omega-3 fatty acids like fish, avocado, walnuts, and olive oil has exceptional benefits for heart health.

Strategically manipulating **carbohydrate** intake through techniques like carb cycling helps manage blood sugar spikes and crashes. Large fluctuations in blood glucose put stress on the cardiovascular system. Keeping blood sugar balanced reduces internal inflammation and the risk of atherosclerosis. Avoiding added or refined sugars is especially important.

Incorporating regular high-intensity interval training **workouts** is phenomenal for boosting cardiovascular fitness. HIIT workouts alternate short bursts of intense activity with recovery periods. This trains the heart to pump more blood with each contraction, increasing its efficiency and capacity over time. Strength training is also beneficial, as additional muscle requires more energy, which increases resting metabolism and cardiovascular function.

Beyond nutrition and exercise, other **lifestyle** factors targeted through a metabolic confusion program enhance heart health. Getting quality sleep allows the cardiovascular system to rejuvenate. Chronic sleep deprivation is linked to an increased risk of heart disease and stroke. Similarly, managing stress properly gives the heart a reprieve from continually elevated stress hormones. Prioritizing recovery through stretching, massage, meditation, and rest days is also beneficial.

Supplements may also support the heart. Omega-3 fish oil, curcumin, coenzyme Q10, and magnesium are all well-researched options. However, nutrition from whole foods should provide the basic foundation. Certain metabolic-enhancing supplements can potentially raise heart rate or blood pressure, so they should be used cautiously.

Over time, the cumulative impact of increased activity, balanced nutrition, managed stress, and ideal body composition creates a profoundly positive **snowball effect** on cardiovascular health. Some benefits happen quickly, while others accumulate gradually. Improved cholesterol panels and blood pressure readings should be noticeable within weeks. Greater endurance and stamina will also be apparent during workouts, indicating enhanced cardiovascular fitness.

However, the long-term effects are arguably more valuable. Individuals who maintain metabolic flexibility and a healthy body composition drastically **reduce** their **risk for heart attack**, **stroke**, and other cardiovascular diseases. The heart is able to function optimally even at rest without excessive strain. Activities can be performed with ease. Essentially, the cardiovascular system reverts to a more youthful state of function.

The metabolic confusion strategies contained in this book thus help enhance both short-term markers of cardiovascular wellness as well as lifelong heart health. Just be sure to discuss significant diet or exercise modifications with your physician, especially if you are currently taking medications for blood pressure, cholesterol, or diabetes. Adjustments may be warranted. With your doctor's consent, you can dramatically improve your cardiovascular health.

Temporary plateaus should not discourage you from losing weight and improving your fitness. Ups and downs are normal. Remain **consistent** with your metabolic, nutrition, and exercise programming, and the cardiovascular benefits will come. Monitor key markers like blood pressure, resting heart rate, cholesterol, endurance, and waist circumference to track results.

Most importantly, **listen to your body**. If you feel excess fatigue, shortness of breath, dizziness, or chest discomfort, stop and consult your physician promptly. Metabolic confusion should make exercise feel easier over time, not harder. This book's recommendations aim to enhance health, not undermine it.

Start today by taking a small step, like going for a 10-minute walk or choosing a salad over a burger for lunch. Build momentum with each additional healthy choice. Before long, your lab tests and energy levels will validate the enhanced cardiovascular function. Your heart will be stronger, your arteries will be clearer, and your vitality will be amplified. Improved cardiovascular health equates to an improved quality of life.

Enhanced Mental Clarity and Mood

The connection between the body and mind is powerful. Strategic metabolic confusion techniques optimize the physical body, thereby enhancing mental performance and emotional health. Losing excess fat, building lean muscle, and achieving metabolic flexibility provide both short- and long-term cognitive benefits.

In the short term, effective nutrition helps stabilize blood sugar, which provides steady **energy** and prevents crashes. Strategic carb intake provides the brain with the glucose it prefers while avoiding spikes and drops. Protein provides essential amino acids that support focus and concentration. Staying hydrated is also key. Even mild dehydration can negatively impact mood and mental clarity.

Getting regular exercise also boosts **mental acuity**. Cardiovascular exercise increases blood flow and oxygen delivery to the brain. Strength training helps elevate neurotransmitters like dopamine and serotonin, which regulate emotions. Just 30 minutes of moderate exercise can immediately sharpen focus, reaction time, and memory. Moving your body makes the mind work better.

Over time, losing excess weight eases inflammation, which can **cloud thinking**. Obesity and chronic high blood sugar contribute to dementia risk later in life. Shedding pounds protects the brain. Dietary components like omega-3s and antioxidants further fight systemic and neural inflammation for **enhanced cognition**.

Increasing lean muscle mass also optimizes **neurotransmitter balance**, which regulates mood. Both cardio and strength training boost the production of feel-good endorphins. Building physical confidence with a strong, capable body also nurtures mental confidence and emotional wellbeing.

Moreover, the discipline required to adhere to strategic nutrition and consistent workouts strengthens **willpower** and **concentration**. Pushing through challenges combats mindless overeating. Goal-setting and tracking progress build accountability. Planning and preparation improve organizational skills. Metabolic confusion requires mental strength.

When focusing on health, mental shifts also occur. Stressors seem less intimidating. Small progress fuels **motivation**. Constructive input replaces negative self-talk. Surrounding yourself with positive people facilitates this mental awakening. You can redirect your previously wasted energy towards solutions.

Potent superfoods like leafy greens, berries, and fatty fish provide compounds that optimize **neural connections**. Intermittent fasting may also aid in the creation of new brain cells. Conversely, highly processed fast food impairs cognition. Clean eating bolsters both the mind and body.

Sleep is essential for cognitive function, as the **brain detoxes** and **regenerates** at night. Conversely, sleep deprivation results in cloudy thinking and emotional instability. Getting quality rest enhances mental clarity.

Supplements like fish oil, turmeric, and magnesium support both short- and long-term **brain health**. Adaptogens can also stabilize mood. However, whole foods and lifestyle strategies should be the foundation.

Over time, the impact of enhanced fitness, balanced nutrition, sufficient sleep, and stress management greatly sharpens **cognition**. The ability to concentrate for long periods improves. Memory and learning capacity increase. Response time quickens. Mental fatigue is reduced. Neurons fire faster, and neural connections strengthen. You essentially rejuvenate your mind.

With increased energy and enhanced cognition, the overall outlook also lifts. **Mood** stabilizes. **Motivation** and **confidence** climb. **Discipline** and **willpower** grow stronger. You notice **solutions** rather than obstacles. You handle stressful events with **calmness** and **clarity**. Every aspect of life improves.

The mind and body are interconnected. When you optimize one, you enhance the other. Metabolic confusion provides the blueprint to maximize physical health and thus elevate mental wellbeing. Sharper thinking, faster reaction times, stabilized moods, and an uplifted outlook will soon become your new normal. Enhanced mental clarity generates enhanced joy and vitality.

Longevity and Metabolic Health

The strategies for enhancing metabolism outlined in this book deliver a powerful boost to overall wellness and vitality. However, the benefits go far beyond just looking and feeling better in the short term. Optimizing metabolic health through proper nutrition, strategic exercise, and supportive lifestyle habits provides anti-aging and longevity benefits that pay dividends over the course of your lifespan.

Research has conclusively demonstrated that individuals who maintain a healthy body weight and composition via balanced eating, regular activity, and metabolic flexibility live **longer lives** with a dramatically **lower risk for chronic disease**. Their cells and tissues remain in a more youthful state longer, which delays the onset of age-related physical and mental decline. This chapter explores the mechanisms through which metabolic health optimization wards off aging and promotes longevity.

First and foremost, maintaining consistent fitness **preserves muscle mass and function** across the lifespan. Progressive strength training is particularly key. Starting as early as age 30, adults can lose 3–5% of muscle mass per decade if inactive. This muscle loss accelerates aging and functional impairment. Preserving lean muscle via nutrition and resistance training maintains strength, mobility, and vitality. Muscular fitness also elevates vital biomarkers of health like growth hormones, which decline with age.

Cardiovascular exercise provides further **anti-aging** effects. Aerobic fitness keeps the heart strong and flexible, preventing stiffening of the arteries. Active individuals have biological markers indicating vascular health up to 15 years younger than their actual age. Cardio workout routines with variation, like those emphasized in this program, maximize these benefits.

Strategically manipulating carbohydrate intake helps to maintain **insulin sensitivity** and optimal **blood sugar regulation** as you age. Chronic high blood sugar and insulin resistance accelerate cellular oxidation, inflammation, and aging. Managing carbohydrates through techniques like nutrient cycling evens out blood sugar spikes, promoting a balanced insulin response. This reduces oxidative stress and systemic inflammation.

Calorie manipulation through intermittent fasting may also trigger the production of longevity compounds. Fasting cues an **adaptive stress response** associated with a longer lifespan in animal models. Periodic calorie restriction acts as a hormetic stressor that strengthens cellular defense systems.

Consuming a diet abundant in whole, unprocessed foods full of antioxidants, polyphenols, fiber, and anti-inflammatory fats provides compounds that combat **free radical damage** and oxidative stress—major factors in aging. In particular, colorful fruits, vegetables, nuts, seeds, fish, and extra virgin olive oil defend against cellular decay.

Sleep is also integral to longevity. Deep sleep activates **cellular repair** and allows metabolic processes to rebalance. Skimping on sleep accelerates biological aging. Getting adequate rest makes anti-aging hormones like melatonin and human growth hormone peak.

Managing stress through techniques like yoga, meditation, and mindfulness also reduces **systemic inflammation** and **cortisol** levels. Environmental toxins, such as cigarette smoke, chemicals, and pollution, also accelerate aging. Reducing exposure and enhancing detoxification pathways help preserve cellular integrity.

Cumulatively, the metabolic confusion techniques and lifestyle choices promoted in this book activate the body's innate anti-aging defenses while preventing disease, dysfunction, and decline. You sustain high energy, ideal body composition, sharp cognition, balanced hormones, and peak performance throughout adulthood and into your senior years.

With consistency, the risk-reducing effects compound exponentially. While one month of healthy habits provides benefits, a lifetime of metabolic flexibility and clean living makes aging gracefully into your 80s, 90s, and beyond an attainable goal. The longevity payoff is substantial for those committed to the lifestyle.

Our society often presents longevity and vitality as being out of our control or based on luck. However, implementing foundational lifestyle choices like balanced nutrition, regular exercise, stress management, and ideal sleep provides incredible influence over the aging process. Take control of your metabolism and cellular health starting today and reap the anti-aging rewards for decades to come.

Increased Physical Endurance

Having the energy, strength, and stamina to complete daily activities with vigor is a key marker of health. Implementing a comprehensive metabolic, nutrition, and exercise program powerfully enhances physical capabilities and endurance. Both in the short and long term, properly fueling your body and incorporating varied fitness routines will enable you to push harder and last longer during any physical task.

In the immediate sense, strategic carbohydrate consumption prior to exercise provides readily **available glucose** that muscles utilize for energy production. This enhances workout capacity and delays fatigue. Protein eaten both before and after training aids in muscle repair and growth. Staying hydrated prevents training-hindering cramps. Good pre-workout fuel lets you maximize each gym session.

Ongoing, eating a balanced diet with adequate calories, macronutrients, and micronutrients ensures your body has the constant **resources** it needs to adapt to regular training. You rebuild stronger instead of breaking down. Sufficient protein intake, coupled with strength training, triggers muscle building and improved endurance.

A diet rich in a variety of whole foods provides minerals like magnesium and iron that are essential for **energy** production, **muscle** contraction, and **oxygen** delivery during activity, avoiding nutritional deficiencies. Deficiencies sap endurance. Adequate intake enhances it.

Engaging in a mixture of resistance training, high-intensity intervals, sustained cardio, and active recovery improves **metabolic** machinery and **cardiorespiratory** fitness. Your heart, lungs, and blood vessels adapt to deliver more oxygen. Muscles enhance their ability to produce energy aerobically. Your engine revs higher.

Incorporating periodic metabolic training techniques like low-carb days, training fasted, or doing targeted two-a-day workouts spurs further rapid fitness gains by **triggering adaptation**. You become adept at flexibly fueling workouts.

As your body composition improves through fat loss and added lean mass, your **strength-to-weight ratio** climbs. Activities require less relative effort. Your engine becomes more powerful. Carrying a lighter load translates to greater endurance.

Recovery practices like sleep, massage, foam rolling, stretching, ice baths, and rest days allow your body to fully **regenerate** instead of remaining in a chronically fatigued state. Proper rest enables progression.

Over time, the cumulative impact of intelligent training, nutrient-dense eating, and balanced recovery potently transforms your **physical capabilities**. Your lungs expand, your muscles strengthen, and your heart adapts. Fitness compounds.

Soon, you'll realize your **previous limits** are now warm-ups. Fatigue occurs later in workouts, if at all. You bounce back faster after exertion. The hills seem flat. Weights feel lighter. Endurance skyrockets.

This enhanced capacity translates to every area of life. Daily tasks like yardwork and playing with kids require less effort. You can hike farther, swim longer, and lift more before hitting exhaustion. Exercise feels easier and more enjoyable.

The techniques for metabolic confusion give you more **control** over your body and abilities. Strategically constructing nutrition and fitness routines allows you to unleash your inner athlete. Your only limits are those of your own mind.

So embrace the small wins day by day. The incremental gains in **strength**, **speed**, **power**, and **endurance** fuel your motivation. Suddenly, you realize months have passed and your capabilities have been transformed. You have become an endurance machine.

Trust the process and make smart choices every day. Soon, heavy will become light, hard will turn easy, and long will grow short. Increased physical endurance creates a positive cycle of empowerment, lifting you to heights previously unfathomable. Your body will amaze you with what it can do.

Maintaining Results Over Time

Committing to permanent lifestyle evolution is key to preserving your hard-earned metabolic flexibility, body composition, and wellness.

The initial excitement and motivation during the intense fat loss and body recomposition phases can sometimes wane once you've reached your goals. Without vigilant maintenance, it is possible to fall back into previous poor habits and gain weight. However, with conscious effort, you can make your new metabolic health and physique your new normal for life.

First and foremost, continue **tracking** your habits and results. Periodically reassess body measurements like weight, body fat percentage, and waist circumference. Also analyze bloodwork, blood pressure, resting heart rate, and other health markers every 3–6 months. Reviewing objective data prevents complacency and motivates continued adherence.

Accept that some weight **fluctuation** is inevitable, so do not obsess over normal ups and downs. Expect to make minor training and nutrition adjustments periodically based on results and changing life circumstances. What worked initially may need to be modified to continue progressing.

Strategically ease out of an aggressive calorie deficit to find your new caloric **equilibrium**, where your weight stabilizes. Increase calories gradually while monitoring changes in weight and body composition. Find your personalized sweet spot.

Similarly, **transition** exercise programming from rapid fat loss to long-term fitness. Reduce training frequency or intensity slightly while still maintaining a high challenge. Prioritize workout consistency above all else, even on busy weeks. Quickly resume missed sessions.

Permanently adopt the **80/20** approach to **eating**. Eighty percent of meals should be whole, single-ingredient foods. The other 20% can be more flexible without consequence. This sustainable balance allows you to reap long-term metabolic benefits without feeling deprived.

Do **not** completely **eliminate foods**. Deprivation inevitably fails. Instead, practice moderation and mindfulness. Enjoy treats occasionally, without guilt. Just be intentional about when and how much. A little dark chocolate or ice cream here and there won't sabotage you.

Develop awareness of **emotional** or situational eating **triggers** so you can differentiate between true hunger and cravings. Practice self-care that does not involve food. Cultivate alternative instant mood boosters like exercise, music, reading, or socializing.

Make **fitness** a **rewarding** experience by participating in activities you genuinely enjoy. Experiment until you find forms of movement you like. Variety prevents boredom. Consider hiring a trainer in the in the short term for accountability and guidance if motivation wanes.

Explore **new** healthy **recipes** and foods so nutrition remains interesting rather than monotonous. To stay inspired, share recipes and meal ideas with friends or health-minded social media groups.

On the calendar, designate periodic **reassessment** weeks to analyze habits and progress. Rededicate yourself to strict adherence during these evaluation weeks. They can be used as tune-ups and resets.

Lifelong metabolic health and leanness are absolutely achievable with mindset shifts from short-term fixes to **permanent** lifestyle evolution. The efforts become easier and more automatic over time. You may occasionally need to recommit and tighten things up, but conscious health and fitness truly can become your default.

Have faith in the cumulative impact of perseverance. Small daily actions stack up to produce incredible results over months and years. Every meal, workout, and health decision matters. Keep your eye on the long game, and you will maintain amazing metabolic wellness for life.

MEAL PLAN

This meal plan is structured to follow a carb cycling approach, alternating between 2 high-carb days and 5 low-carb days each week. This method is specifically designed to support weight loss while optimizing energy levels and metabolic function. All the recipes included can be found in the bonus section.

	Week 1	Week 2
Day 1 (High-Carb Day)	**Breakfast**: Banana Berry Oatmeal **Lunch**: Chickpea Power Salad Bowl **Dinner**: Veggie-fried Brown Rice with Tofu and Cashews **Snacks/Desserts**: Banana Nut Energy Bites, Berry Yogurt Parfait Cups	**Breakfast**: Whole Grain Toast **Lunch**: Falafel Wrap **Dinner**: Cajun Shrimp and Sausage over Creamy Polenta **Snacks/Desserts**: Granola Yogurt Parfait, Peanut Butter Banana Smoothie
Day 2 (High-Carb Day)	**Breakfast**: Pancakes with Fresh Berries **Lunch**: Quinoa Buddha Bowl **Dinner**: Quinoa-stuffed Peppers with Ground Turkey and Cheese **Snacks/Desserts**: Quinoa Fruit Salad, Sweet Potato Toast Rounds	**Breakfast**: Sweet Potato Veggie Omelet **Lunch**: Waldorf Chicken Salad **Dinner**: Vegetarian Chili Mac with Whole Wheat Pasta and Beans **Snacks/Desserts**: Energizing Breakfast Tacos, Trail Mix Protein Bars
Day 3 (Low-Carb Day)	**Breakfast**: Spinach and Feta Omelet **Lunch**: Tuna Lettuce Wraps **Dinner**: Grilled Salmon with Zucchini Noodles and Pesto **Snacks/Desserts**: Cucumber Avocado Roll-Ups, Parmesan Zucchini Chips	**Breakfast**: Bacon and Egg Muffin Cups **Lunch**: Chicken Mason Jar Salad **Dinner**: Turkey Bacon-wrapped Asparagus Bundles **Snacks/Desserts**: Prosciutto-Wrapped Asparagus Spears, Bell Pepper Nachos
Day 4 (Low-Carb Day)	**Breakfast**: Veggie Egg Cup Muffins **Lunch**: Chicken Soup **Dinner**: Chicken Cabbage Stir-fry with Coconut Aminos **Snacks/Desserts**: Egg Salad Stuffed Cherry Tomatoes, Crispy Kale Chips	**Breakfast**: Chia Coconut Pudding Parfait **Lunch**: Chopped Veggie Salad **Dinner**: Cheeseburger Salad with Lettuce, Tomato, and Pickles **Snacks/Desserts**: Avocado Egg Salad, Spicy Roasted Edamame
Day 5 (Low-Carb Day)	**Breakfast**: Protein-Packed Green Smoothie **Lunch**: Steak Salad **Dinner**: Taco Salad with Ground Beef, Romaine, Avocado, and Salsa **Snacks/Desserts**: Cheese and Pepperoni Bites, Avocado Deviled Eggs	**Breakfast**: Cottage Cheese Power Bowl **Lunch**: Roasted Chicken Wrap **Dinner**: Steak Fajita Bowls **Snacks/Desserts**: Greek Salad with Grilled Shrimp, Oven-Baked Cinnamon Apple Chips
Day 6 (Low-Carb Day)	**Breakfast**: Smoked Salmon Avocado Toast **Lunch**: Mason Jar Salad **Dinner**: Meatballs with Roasted Cauliflower Mash and Marinara **Snacks/Desserts**: Smoked Salmon Cucumber Rolls, Stuffed Celery Sticks	**Breakfast**: Smoked Salmon Avocado Toast **Lunch**: Zucchini Noodle Pasta Salad **Dinner**: Salmon Spinach Salad **Snacks/Desserts**: Turkey and Avocado Lettuce Wraps, Whole Grain Crackers with Avocado Hummus
Day 7 (Low-Carb Day)	**Breakfast**: Zucchini Noodles with Pesto Chicken **Lunch**: Cauliflower Fried Rice **Dinner**: Shrimp and Vegetable Kabobs served with Cauliflower Rice **Snacks/Desserts**: Cottage Cheese Stuffed Mini Peppers, Tuna Cucumber Boats	**Breakfast**: Coconut Flour Pancakes **Lunch**: Mason Jar Salad **Dinner**: Zucchini Lasagna **Snacks/Desserts**: Cauliflower Hummus with Veggie Sticks, Parmesan Zucchini Chips

	Week 3	Week 4
Day 1 (High-Carb Day)	**Breakfast**: Fruit and Nut Oats **Lunch**: Quinoa Protein Power Bowl **Dinner**: Eggplant Parmesan served over Whole Wheat Pasta with Tomato Sauce **Snacks/Desserts**: Banana Nut Energy Bites, Greek Yogurt Dip with Fresh Fruit Slices	**Breakfast**: Whole Grain Waffle **Lunch**: Chickpea Power Salad Bowl **Dinner**: Vegetarian Chili Mac with Whole Wheat Pasta and Beans **Snacks/Desserts**: Peanut Butter Banana Smoothie, Trail Mix Protein Bars
Day 2 (High-Carb Day)	**Breakfast**: Pancakes with Fresh Berries **Lunch**: Tuna Pasta Salad **Dinner**: Sweet Potato Shepherd's Pie **Snacks/Desserts**: Berry Yogurt Parfait Cups, Mini Veggie Pita Pockets	**Breakfast**: Granola Yogurt Parfait **Lunch**: Falafel Wrap **Dinner**: Greek Turkey Burger served with Sweet Potato Fries and Tzatziki **Snacks/Desserts**: Berry Yogurt Parfait Cups, Mini Veggie Pita Pockets
Day 3 (Low-Carb Day)	**Breakfast**: Veggie Egg Cup Muffins **Lunch**: Chicken Soup **Dinner**: Quinoa Fried Rice **Snacks/Desserts**: Stuffed Celery Sticks, Spicy Roasted Edamame	**Breakfast**: Spinach and Feta Omelet **Lunch**: Roasted Chicken Wrap **Dinner**: Steak Fajita Bowls **Snacks/Desserts**: Parmesan Zucchini Chips, Cucumber Avocado Roll-Ups
Day 4 (Low-Carb Day)	**Breakfast**: Protein-Packed Green Smoothie **Lunch**: Taco Salad with Ground Beef, Romaine, Avocado, and Salsa **Dinner**: Lentil Sloppy Joes **Snacks/Desserts**: Crispy Kale Chips, Avocado Deviled Eggs	**Breakfast**: Zucchini Noodles with Pesto Chicken **Lunch**: Mason Jar Salad **Dinner**: Salmon Spinach Salad **Snacks/Desserts**: Tuna Cucumber Boats, Stuffed Celery Sticks
Day 5 (Low-Carb Day)	**Breakfast**: Bacon and Egg Muffin Cups **Lunch**: Grilled Salmon with Zucchini Noodles and Pesto **Dinner**: Meatloaf Muffins **Snacks/Desserts**: Parmesan Zucchini Chips, Cucumber Avocado Roll-Ups	**Breakfast**: Cottage Cheese Power Bowl **Lunch**: Egg Salad Cups **Dinner**: Zucchini Lasagna **Snacks/Desserts**: Spicy Roasted Edamame, Avocado Deviled Eggs
Day 6 (Low-Carb Day)	**Breakfast**: Coconut Flour Pancakes **Lunch**: Greek Salad with Grilled Shrimp **Dinner**: Quinoa Lasagna **Snacks/Desserts**: Tuna Cucumber Boats, Sweet Potato Toast Rounds	**Breakfast**: Veggie Egg Cup Muffins **Lunch**: Grilled Salmon with Zucchini Noodles and Pesto **Dinner**: Quinoa Fried Rice **Snacks/Desserts**: Crispy Kale Chips, Bell Pepper Nachos
Day 7 (Low-Carb Day)	**Breakfast**: Cottage Cheese Power Bowl **Lunch**: Chicken Caesar Lettuce Wraps **Dinner**: Cauliflower Crust Pizza topped with Tomato Sauce, Mozzarella, and Pepperoni **Snacks/Desserts**: Bell Pepper Nachos, Oven-Baked Cinnamon Apple Chips	**Breakfast**: Protein-Packed Green Smoothie **Lunch**: Chicken Caesar Lettuce Wraps **Dinner**: Cauliflower Crust Pizza topped with Tomato Sauce, Mozzarella, and Pepperoni **Snacks/Desserts**: Parmesan Zucchini Chips, Oven-Baked Cinnamon Apple Chips

	Week 5	**Week 6**
Day 1 (High-Carb Day)	**Breakfast**: Banana Berry Oatmeal **Lunch**: Loaded Baked Sweet Potato **Dinner**: Veggie-fried Brown Rice with Tofu and Cashews **Snacks/Desserts**: Peanut Butter Banana Smoothie, Whole Grain Crackers with Avocado Hummus	**Breakfast**: Whole Grain Toast **Lunch**: Chickpea Power Salad Bowl **Dinner**: Cajun Shrimp and Sausage over Creamy Polenta **Snacks/Desserts**: Banana Nut Energy Bites, Berry Yogurt Parfait Cups
Day 2 (High-Carb Day)	**Breakfast**: Pancakes with Fresh Berries **Lunch**: Quinoa Protein Power Bowl **Dinner**: Greek Turkey Burger served with Sweet Potato Fries and Tzatziki **Snacks/Desserts**: Berry Yogurt Parfait Cups, Mini Veggie Pita Pockets	**Breakfast**: Granola Yogurt Parfait **Lunch**: Quinoa Buddha Bowl **Dinner**: Vegetarian Chili Mac with Whole Wheat Pasta and Beans **Snacks/Desserts**: Quinoa Fruit Salad, Sweet Potato Toast Rounds
Day 3 (Low-Carb Day)	**Breakfast**: Spinach and Feta Omelet **Lunch**: Tuna Lettuce Wraps **Dinner**: Grilled Salmon with Zucchini Noodles and Pesto **Snacks/Desserts**: Parmesan Zucchini Chips, Stuffed Celery Sticks	**Breakfast**: Veggie Egg Cup Muffins **Lunch**: Tuna Lettuce Wraps **Dinner**: Grilled Salmon with Zucchini Noodles and Pesto **Snacks/Desserts**: Parmesan Zucchini Chips, Stuffed Celery Sticks
Day 4 (Low-Carb Day)	**Breakfast**: Chia Coconut Pudding Parfait **Lunch**: Chicken Soup **Dinner**: Taco Salad with Ground Beef, Romaine, Avocado, and Salsa **Snacks/Desserts**: Crispy Kale Chips, Avocado Deviled Eggs	**Breakfast**: Chia Coconut Pudding Parfait **Lunch**: Chicken Soup **Dinner**: Taco Salad with Ground Beef, Romaine, Avocado, and Salsa **Snacks/Desserts**: Crispy Kale Chips, Avocado Deviled Eggs
Day 5 (Low-Carb Day)	**Breakfast**: Veggie Egg Cup Muffins **Lunch**: Zucchini Noodle Pasta Salad **Dinner**: Meatballs with Roasted Cauliflower Mash and Marinara **Snacks/Desserts**: Cucumber Avocado Roll-Ups, Bell Pepper Nachos	**Breakfast**: Spinach and Feta Omelet **Lunch**: Zucchini Noodle Pasta Salad **Dinner**: Meatballs with Roasted Cauliflower Mash and Marinara **Snacks/Desserts**: Cucumber Avocado Roll-Ups, Bell Pepper Nachos
Day 6 (Low-Carb Day)	**Breakfast**: Smoked Salmon Avocado Toast **Lunch**: Cauliflower Fried Rice **Dinner**: Turkey Bacon-wrapped Asparagus Bundles **Snacks/Desserts**: Cottage Cheese Stuffed Mini Peppers, Oven-Baked Cinnamon Apple Chips	**Breakfast**: Smoked Salmon Avocado Toast **Lunch**: Cauliflower Fried Rice **Dinner**: Turkey Bacon-wrapped Asparagus Bundles **Snacks/Desserts**: Cottage Cheese Stuffed Mini Peppers, Oven-Baked Cinnamon Apple Chips
Day 7 (Low-Carb Day)	**Breakfast**: Bacon and Egg Muffin Cups **Lunch**: Greek Salad with Grilled Shrimp **Dinner**: Chicken Avocado Boat **Snacks/Desserts**: Spicy Roasted Edamame, Parmesan Zucchini Chips	**Breakfast**: Bacon and Egg Muffin Cups **Lunch**: Greek Salad with Grilled Shrimp **Dinner**: Chicken Avocado Boat **Snacks/Desserts**: Spicy Roasted Edamame, Parmesan Zucchini Chips

	Week 7	Week 8
Day 1 (High-Carb Day)	**Breakfast**: Pancakes with Fresh Berries **Lunch**: Loaded Baked Sweet Potato **Dinner**: Veggie-fried Brown Rice with Tofu and Cashews **Snacks/Desserts**: Banana Nut Energy Bites, Berry Yogurt Parfait Cups	**Breakfast**: Quinoa Breakfast Bowl **Lunch**: Falafel Wrap **Dinner**: Vegetarian Chili Mac with Whole Wheat Pasta and Beans **Snacks/Desserts**: Banana Nut Energy Bites, Berry Yogurt Parfait Cups
Day 2 (High-Carb Day)	**Breakfast**: Fruit and Nut Oats **Lunch**: Quinoa Protein Power Bowl **Dinner**: Greek Turkey Burger served with Sweet Potato Fries and Tzatziki **Snacks/Desserts**: Quinoa Fruit Salad, Sweet Potato Toast Rounds	**Breakfast**: Whole Grain Waffle **Lunch**: Chickpea Power Salad Bowl **Dinner**: Eggplant Parmesan served over Whole Wheat Pasta with Tomato Sauce **Snacks/Desserts**: Sweet Potato Toast Rounds, Whole Grain Crackers with Avocado Hummus
Day 3 (Low-Carb Day)	**Breakfast**: Veggie Egg Cup Muffins **Lunch**: Tuna Lettuce Wraps **Dinner**: Grilled Salmon with Zucchini Noodles and Pesto **Snacks/Desserts**: Parmesan Zucchini Chips, Stuffed Celery Sticks	**Breakfast**: Prosciutto-Wrapped Asparagus Spears **Lunch**: Chicken Soup **Dinner**: Grilled Salmon with Zucchini Noodles and Pesto **Snacks/Desserts**: Avocado Deviled Eggs, Parmesan Zucchini Chips
Day 4 (Low-Carb Day)	**Breakfast**: Chia Coconut Pudding Parfait **Lunch**: Chicken Soup **Dinner**: Taco Salad with Ground Beef, Romaine, Avocado, and Salsa **Snacks/Desserts**: Crispy Kale Chips, Avocado Deviled Eggs	**Breakfast**: Veggie Egg Cup Muffins **Lunch**: Zucchini Noodle Pasta Salad **Dinner**: Taco Salad with Ground Beef, Romaine, Avocado, and Salsa **Snacks/Desserts**: Cucumber Avocado Roll-Ups, Crispy Kale Chips
Day 5 (Low-Carb Day)	**Breakfast**: Spinach and Feta Omelet **Lunch**: Zucchini Noodle Pasta Salad **Dinner**: Meatballs with Roasted Cauliflower Mash and Marinara **Snacks/Desserts**: Cucumber Avocado Roll-Ups, Bell Pepper Nachos	**Breakfast**: Cottage Cheese Power Bowl **Lunch**: Chicken Caesar Lettuce Wraps **Dinner**: Cheeseburger Salad with Lettuce, Tomato, and Pickles **Snacks/Desserts**: Bell Pepper Nachos, Stuffed Celery Sticks
Day 6 (Low-Carb Day)	**Breakfast**: Smoked Salmon Avocado Toast **Lunch**: Cauliflower Fried Rice **Dinner**: Turkey Bacon-wrapped Asparagus Bundles **Snacks/Desserts**: Cottage Cheese Stuffed Mini Peppers, Oven-Baked Cinnamon Apple Chips	**Breakfast**: Bacon and Egg Muffin Cups **Lunch**: Greek Salad with Grilled Shrimp **Dinner**: Steak Fajita Bowls **Snacks/Desserts**: Smoked Salmon Cucumber Bites, Tuna Cucumber Boats
Day 7 (Low-Carb Day)	**Breakfast**: Bacon and Egg Muffin Cups **Lunch**: Greek Salad with Grilled Shrimp **Dinner**: Chicken Avocado Boat **Snacks/Desserts**: Spicy Roasted Edamame, Parmesan Zucchini Chips	**Breakfast**: Spinach and Feta Omelet **Lunch**: Cauliflower Fried Rice **Dinner**: Shrimp and Vegetable Kabobs served with Cauliflower Rice **Snacks/Desserts**: Spicy Roasted Edamame, Mini Veggie Pita Pockets

	Week 9	Week 10
Day 1 (High-Carb Day)	**Breakfast**: Pancakes with Fresh Berries **Lunch**: Quinoa Buddha Bowl **Dinner**: Cajun Shrimp and Sausage over Creamy Polenta **Snacks/Desserts**: Banana Nut Energy Bites, Berry Yogurt Parfait Cups	**Breakfast**: Whole Grain Toast **Lunch**: Falafel Wrap **Dinner**: Cajun Shrimp and Sausage over Creamy Polenta **Snacks/Desserts**: Granola Yogurt Parfait, Peanut Butter Banana Smoothie
Day 2 (High-Carb Day)	**Breakfast**: Granola Yogurt Parfait **Lunch**: Loaded Baked Sweet Potato **Dinner**: Greek Turkey Burger served with Sweet Potato Fries and Tzatziki **Snacks/Desserts**: Sweet Potato Toast Rounds, Peanut Butter Banana Smoothie	**Breakfast**: Sweet Potato Veggie Omelet **Lunch**: Waldorf Chicken Salad **Dinner**: Eggplant Parmesan served over Whole Wheat Pasta with Tomato Sauce **Snacks/Desserts**: Energizing Breakfast Tacos, Trail Mix Protein Bars
Day 3 (Low-Carb Day)	**Breakfast**: Veggie Egg Cup Muffins **Lunch**: Chicken Soup **Dinner**: Grilled Salmon with Zucchini Noodles and Pesto **Snacks/Desserts**: Avocado Deviled Eggs, Parmesan Zucchini Chips	**Breakfast**: Smoked Salmon Avocado Toast **Lunch**: Zucchini Noodle Pasta Salad **Dinner**: Turkey Bacon-wrapped Asparagus Bundles **Snacks/Desserts**: Spicy Roasted Edamame, Avocado Deviled Eggs
Day 4 (Low-Carb Day)	**Breakfast**: Cottage Cheese Power Bowl **Lunch**: Chicken Caesar Lettuce Wraps **Dinner**: Cheeseburger Salad with Lettuce, Tomato, and Pickles **Snacks/Desserts**: Bell Pepper Nachos, Stuffed Celery Sticks	**Breakfast**: Cottage Cheese Power Bowl **Lunch**: Roasted Chicken Wrap **Dinner**: Steak Fajita Bowls **Snacks/Desserts**: Greek Salad with Grilled Shrimp, Oven-Baked Cinnamon Apple Chips
Day 5 (Low-Carb Day)	**Breakfast**: Veggie Egg Cup Muffins **Lunch**: Steak Salad **Dinner**: Taco Salad with Ground Beef, Romaine, Avocado, and Salsa **Snacks/Desserts**: Cheese and Pepperoni Bites, Avocado Deviled Eggs	**Breakfast**: Zucchini Noodles with Pesto Chicken **Lunch**: Mason Jar Salad **Dinner**: Salmon Spinach Salad **Snacks/Desserts**: Tuna Cucumber Boats, Stuffed Celery Sticks
Day 6 (Low-Carb Day)	**Breakfast**: Protein-Packed Green Smoothie **Lunch**: Chicken Mason Jar Salad **Dinner**: Meatballs with Roasted Cauliflower Mash and Marinara **Snacks/Desserts**: Smoked Salmon Cucumber Rolls, Stuffed Celery Sticks	**Breakfast**: Coconut Flour Pancakes **Lunch**: Mason Jar Salad **Dinner**: Zucchini Lasagna **Snacks/Desserts**: Cauliflower Hummus with Veggie Sticks, Parmesan Zucchini Chips
Day 7 (Low-Carb Day)	**Breakfast**: Bacon and Egg Muffin Cups **Lunch**: Greek Salad with Grilled Shrimp **Dinner**: Shrimp and Vegetable Kabobs served with Cauliflower Rice **Snacks/Desserts**: Parmesan Zucchini Chips, Tuna Cucumber Boats	**Breakfast**: Chia Coconut Pudding Parfait **Lunch**: Chicken Soup **Dinner**: Chicken Cabbage Stir-fry with Coconut Aminos **Snacks/Desserts**: Egg Salad Stuffed Cherry Tomatoes, Crispy Kale Chips

	Week 11	Week 12
Day 1 (High-Carb Day)	**Breakfast**: Fruit and Nut Oats **Lunch**: Quinoa Protein Power Bowl **Dinner**: Eggplant Parmesan served over Whole Wheat Pasta with Tomato Sauce **Snacks/Desserts**: Banana Nut Energy Bites, Greek Yogurt Dip with Fresh Fruit Slices	**Breakfast**: Whole Grain Waffle **Lunch**: Chickpea Power Salad Bowl **Dinner**: Vegetarian Chili Mac with Whole Wheat Pasta and Beans **Snacks/Desserts**: Peanut Butter Banana Smoothie, Trail Mix Protein Bars
Day 2 (High-Carb Day)	**Breakfast**: Pancakes with Fresh Berries **Lunch**: Tuna Pasta Salad **Dinner**: Sweet Potato Shepherd's Pie **Snacks/Desserts**: Berry Yogurt Parfait Cups, Mini Veggie Pita Pockets	**Breakfast**: Granola Yogurt Parfait **Lunch**: Falafel Wrap **Dinner**: Greek Turkey Burger served with Sweet Potato Fries and Tzatziki **Snacks/Desserts**: Berry Yogurt Parfait Cups, Mini Veggie Pita Pockets
Day 3 (Low-Carb Day)	**Breakfast**: Veggie Egg Cup Muffins **Lunch**: Chicken Soup **Dinner**: Quinoa Fried Rice **Snacks/Desserts**: Stuffed Celery Sticks, Spicy Roasted Edamame	**Breakfast**: Spinach and Feta Omelet **Lunch**: Roasted Chicken Wrap **Dinner**: Steak Fajita Bowls **Snacks/Desserts**: Parmesan Zucchini Chips, Cucumber Avocado Roll-Ups
Day 4 (Low-Carb Day)	**Breakfast**: Protein-Packed Green Smoothie **Lunch**: Taco Salad with Ground Beef, Romaine, Avocado, and Salsa **Dinner**: Lentil Sloppy Joes **Snacks/Desserts**: Crispy Kale Chips, Avocado Deviled Eggs	**Breakfast**: Zucchini Noodles with Pesto Chicken **Lunch**: Mason Jar Salad **Dinner**: Salmon Spinach Salad **Snacks/Desserts**: Tuna Cucumber Boats, Stuffed Celery Sticks
Day 5 (Low-Carb Day)	**Breakfast**: Bacon and Egg Muffin Cups **Lunch**: Grilled Salmon with Zucchini Noodles and Pesto **Dinner**: Meatloaf Muffins **Snacks/Desserts**: Parmesan Zucchini Chips, Cucumber Avocado Roll-Ups	**Breakfast**: Cottage Cheese Power Bowl **Lunch**: Egg Salad Cups **Dinner**: Zucchini Lasagna **Snacks/Desserts**: Spicy Roasted Edamame, Avocado Deviled Eggs
Day 6 (Low-Carb Day)	**Breakfast**: Coconut Flour Pancakes **Lunch**: Greek Salad with Grilled Shrimp **Dinner**: Quinoa Lasagna **Snacks/Desserts**: Tuna Cucumber Boats, Sweet Potato Toast Rounds	**Breakfast**: Veggie Egg Cup Muffins **Lunch**: Grilled Salmon with Zucchini Noodles and Pesto **Dinner**: Quinoa Fried Rice **Snacks/Desserts**: Crispy Kale Chips, Bell Pepper Nachos
Day 7 (Low-Carb Day)	**Breakfast**: Cottage Cheese Power Bowl **Lunch**: Chicken Caesar Lettuce Wraps **Dinner**: Cauliflower Crust Pizza topped with Tomato Sauce, Mozzarella, and Pepperoni **Snacks/Desserts**: Bell Pepper Nachos, Oven-Baked Cinnamon Apple Chips	**Breakfast**: Protein-Packed Green Smoothie **Lunch**: Chicken Caesar Lettuce Wraps **Dinner**: Cauliflower Crust Pizza topped with Tomato Sauce, Mozzarella, and Pepperoni **Snacks/Desserts**: Parmesan Zucchini Chips, Oven-Baked Cinnamon Apple Chips

	Week 13	Week 14
Day 1 (High-Carb Day)	**Breakfast**: Banana Berry Oatmeal **Lunch**: Loaded Baked Sweet Potato **Dinner**: Veggie-fried Brown Rice with Tofu and Cashews **Snacks/Desserts**: Peanut Butter Banana Smoothie, Whole Grain Crackers with Avocado Hummus	**Breakfast**: Whole Grain Toast **Lunch**: Chickpea Power Salad Bowl **Dinner**: Cajun Shrimp and Sausage over Creamy Polenta **Snacks/Desserts**: Banana Nut Energy Bites, Berry Yogurt Parfait Cups
Day 2 (High-Carb Day)	**Breakfast**: Pancakes with Fresh Berries **Lunch**: Quinoa Protein Power Bowl **Dinner**: Greek Turkey Burger served with Sweet Potato Fries and Tzatziki **Snacks/Desserts**: Berry Yogurt Parfait Cups, Mini Veggie Pita Pockets	**Breakfast**: Granola Yogurt Parfait **Lunch**: Quinoa Buddha Bowl **Dinner**: Vegetarian Chili Mac with Whole Wheat Pasta and Beans **Snacks/Desserts**: Quinoa Fruit Salad, Sweet Potato Toast Rounds
Day 3 (Low-Carb Day)	**Breakfast**: Spinach and Feta Omelet **Lunch**: Tuna Lettuce Wraps **Dinner**: Grilled Salmon with Zucchini Noodles and Pesto **Snacks/Desserts**: Parmesan Zucchini Chips, Stuffed Celery Sticks	**Breakfast**: Veggie Egg Cup Muffins **Lunch**: Tuna Lettuce Wraps **Dinner**: Grilled Salmon with Zucchini Noodles and Pesto **Snacks/Desserts**: Parmesan Zucchini Chips, Stuffed Celery Sticks
Day 4 (Low-Carb Day)	**Breakfast**: Chia Coconut Pudding Parfait **Lunch**: Chicken Soup **Dinner**: Taco Salad with Ground Beef, Romaine, Avocado, and Salsa **Snacks/Desserts**: Crispy Kale Chips, Avocado Deviled Eggs	**Breakfast**: Chia Coconut Pudding Parfait **Lunch**: Chicken Soup **Dinner**: Taco Salad with Ground Beef, Romaine, Avocado, and Salsa **Snacks/Desserts**: Crispy Kale Chips, Avocado Deviled Eggs
Day 5 (Low-Carb Day)	**Breakfast**: Veggie Egg Cup Muffins **Lunch**: Zucchini Noodle Pasta Salad **Dinner**: Meatballs with Roasted Cauliflower Mash and Marinara **Snacks/Desserts**: Cucumber Avocado Roll-Ups, Bell Pepper Nachos	**Breakfast**: Spinach and Feta Omelet **Lunch**: Zucchini Noodle Pasta Salad **Dinner**: Meatballs with Roasted Cauliflower Mash and Marinara **Snacks/Desserts**: Cucumber Avocado Roll-Ups, Bell Pepper Nachos
Day 6 (Low-Carb Day)	**Breakfast**: Smoked Salmon Avocado Toast **Lunch**: Cauliflower Fried Rice **Dinner**: Turkey Bacon-wrapped Asparagus Bundles **Snacks/Desserts**: Cottage Cheese Stuffed Mini Peppers, Oven-Baked Cinnamon Apple Chips	**Breakfast**: Smoked Salmon Avocado Toast **Lunch**: Cauliflower Fried Rice **Dinner**: Turkey Bacon-wrapped Asparagus Bundles **Snacks/Desserts**: Cottage Cheese Stuffed Mini Peppers, Oven-Baked Cinnamon Apple Chips
Day 7 (Low-Carb Day)	**Breakfast**: Bacon and Egg Muffin Cups **Lunch**: Greek Salad with Grilled Shrimp **Dinner**: Chicken Avocado Boat **Snacks/Desserts**: Spicy Roasted Edamame, Parmesan Zucchini Chips	**Breakfast**: Bacon and Egg Muffin Cups **Lunch**: Greek Salad with Grilled Shrimp **Dinner**: Chicken Avocado Boat **Snacks/Desserts**: Spicy Roasted Edamame, Parmesan Zucchini Chips

	Week 15	Week 16
Day 1 (High-Carb Day)	**Breakfast**: Banana Berry Oatmeal **Lunch**: Chickpea Power Salad Bowl **Dinner**: Veggie-fried Brown Rice with Tofu and Cashews **Snacks/Desserts**: Banana Nut Energy Bites, Berry Yogurt Parfait Cups	**Breakfast**: Pancakes with Fresh Berries **Lunch**: Waldorf Chicken Salad **Dinner**: Greek Turkey Burger served with Sweet Potato Fries and Tzatziki **Snacks/Desserts**: Granola Yogurt Parfait, Peanut Butter Banana Smoothie
Day 2 (High-Carb Day)	**Breakfast**: Whole Grain Toast **Lunch**: Quinoa Buddha Bowl **Dinner**: Cajun Shrimp and Sausage over Creamy Polenta **Snacks/Desserts**: Sweet Potato Toast Rounds, Peanut Butter Banana Smoothie	**Breakfast**: Sweet Potato Veggie Omelet **Lunch**: Quinoa Protein Power Bowl **Dinner**: Vegetarian Chili Mac with Whole Wheat Pasta and Beans **Snacks/Desserts**: Berry Yogurt Parfait Cups, Mini Veggie Pita Pockets
Day 3 (Low-Carb Day)	**Breakfast**: Spinach and Feta Omelet **Lunch**: Tuna Lettuce Wraps **Dinner**: Grilled Salmon with Zucchini Noodles and Pesto **Snacks/Desserts**: Parmesan Zucchini Chips, Stuffed Celery Sticks	**Breakfast**: Smoked Salmon Avocado Toast **Lunch**: Chicken Caesar Lettuce Wraps **Dinner**: Cauliflower Crust Pizza topped with Tomato Sauce, Mozzarella, and Pepperoni **Snacks/Desserts**: Parmesan Zucchini Chips, Tuna Cucumber Boats
Day 4 (Low-Carb Day)	**Breakfast**: Chia Coconut Pudding Parfait **Lunch**: Chicken Soup **Dinner**: Taco Salad with Ground Beef, Romaine, Avocado, and Salsa **Snacks/Desserts**: Crispy Kale Chips, Avocado Deviled Eggs	**Breakfast**: Cottage Cheese Power Bowl **Lunch**: Roasted Chicken Wrap **Dinner**: Quinoa Fried Rice **Snacks/Desserts**: Spicy Roasted Edamame, Avocado Deviled Eggs
Day 5 (Low-Carb Day)	**Breakfast**: Veggie Egg Cup Muffins **Lunch**: Steak Salad **Dinner**: Meatballs with Roasted Cauliflower Mash and Marinara **Snacks/Desserts**: Cucumber Avocado Roll-Ups, Bell Pepper Nachos	**Breakfast**: Veggie Egg Cup Muffins **Lunch**: Chopped Veggie Salad **Dinner**: Steak Fajita Bowls **Snacks/Desserts**: Crispy Kale Chips, Stuffed Celery Sticks
Day 6 (Low-Carb Day)	**Breakfast**: Protein-Packed Green Smoothie **Lunch**: Chicken Mason Jar Salad **Dinner**: Turkey Bacon-wrapped Asparagus Bundles **Snacks/Desserts**: Prosciutto-Wrapped Asparagus Spears, Bell Pepper Nachos	**Breakfast**: Zucchini Noodles with Pesto Chicken **Lunch**: Chicken Mason Jar Salad **Dinner**: Salmon Spinach Salad **Snacks/Desserts**: Tuna Cucumber Boats, Bell Pepper Nachos
Day 7 (Low-Carb Day)	**Breakfast**: Bacon and Egg Muffin Cups **Lunch**: Zucchini Noodle Pasta Salad **Dinner**: Shrimp and Vegetable Kabobs served with Cauliflower Rice **Snacks/Desserts**: Cheese and Pepperoni Bites, Smoked Salmon Cucumber Bites	**Breakfast**: Chia Coconut Pudding Parfait **Lunch**: Zucchini Noodle Pasta Salad **Dinner**: Meatloaf Muffins **Snacks/Desserts**: Avocado Deviled Eggs, Spicy Roasted Edamame

Week 17

Day 1 (High-Carb Day)
Breakfast: Fruit and Nut Oats
Lunch: Quinoa Protein Power Bowl
Dinner: Eggplant Parmesan served over Whole Wheat Pasta with Tomato Sauce
Snacks/Desserts: Banana Nut Energy Bites, Greek Yogurt Dip with Fresh Fruit Slices

Day 2 (High-Carb Day)
Breakfast: Pancakes with Fresh Berries
Lunch: Tuna Pasta Salad
Dinner: Sweet Potato Shepherd's Pie
Snacks/Desserts: Berry Yogurt Parfait Cups, Mini Veggie Pita Pockets

Day 3 (Low-Carb Day)
Breakfast: Veggie Egg Cup Muffins
Lunch: Chicken Soup
Dinner: Quinoa Fried Rice
Snacks/Desserts: Stuffed Celery Sticks, Spicy Roasted Edamame

Day 4 (Low-Carb Day)
Breakfast: Protein-Packed Green Smoothie
Lunch: Taco Salad with Ground Beef, Romaine, Avocado, and Salsa
Dinner: Lentil Sloppy Joes
Snacks/Desserts: Crispy Kale Chips, Avocado Deviled Eggs

Day 5 (Low-Carb Day)
Breakfast: Bacon and Egg Muffin Cups
Lunch: Grilled Salmon with Zucchini Noodles and Pesto
Dinner: Meatloaf Muffins
Snacks/Desserts: Parmesan Zucchini Chips, Cucumber Avocado Roll-Ups

Day 6 (Low-Carb Day)
Breakfast: Coconut Flour Pancakes
Lunch: Greek Salad with Grilled Shrimp
Dinner: Quinoa Lasagna
Snacks/Desserts: Tuna Cucumber Boats, Sweet Potato Toast Rounds

Day 7 (Low-Carb Day)
Breakfast: Cottage Cheese Power Bowl
Lunch: Chicken Caesar Lettuce Wraps
Dinner: Cauliflower Crust Pizza topped with Tomato Sauce, Mozzarella, and Pepperoni
Snacks/Desserts: Bell Pepper Nachos, Oven-Baked Cinnamon Apple Chips

Week 18

Day 1 (High-Carb Day)
Breakfast: Banana Berry Oatmeal
Lunch: Chickpea Power Salad Bowl
Dinner: Veggie-fried Brown Rice with Tofu and Cashews
Snacks/Desserts: Banana Nut Energy Bites, Berry Yogurt Parfait Cups

Day 2 (High-Carb Day)
Breakfast: Whole Grain Toast
Lunch: Falafel Wrap
Dinner: Cajun Shrimp and Sausage over Creamy Polenta
Snacks/Desserts: Energizing Breakfast Tacos, Trail Mix Protein Bars

Day 3 (Low-Carb Day)
Breakfast: Chia Coconut Pudding Parfait
Lunch: Chopped Veggie Salad
Dinner: Cheeseburger Salad with Lettuce, Tomato, and Pickles
Snacks/Desserts: Avocado Egg Salad, Spicy Roasted Edamame

Day 4 (Low-Carb Day)
Breakfast: Bacon and Egg Muffin Cups
Lunch: Grilled Salmon with Zucchini Noodles and Pesto
Dinner: Meatloaf Muffins
Snacks/Desserts: Parmesan Zucchini Chips, Cucumber Avocado Roll-Ups

Day 5 (Low-Carb Day)
Breakfast: Smoked Salmon Avocado Toast
Lunch: Cauliflower Fried Rice
Dinner: Turkey Bacon-wrapped Asparagus Bundles
Snacks/Desserts: Cottage Cheese Stuffed Mini Peppers, Oven-Baked Cinnamon Apple Chips

Day 6 (Low-Carb Day)
Breakfast: Spinach and Feta Omelet
Lunch: Zucchini Noodle Pasta Salad
Dinner: Meatballs with Roasted Cauliflower Mash and Marinara
Snacks/Desserts: Cucumber Avocado Roll-Ups, Bell Pepper Nachos

Day 7 (Low-Carb Day)
Breakfast: Cottage Cheese Power Bowl
Lunch: Chicken Caesar Lettuce Wraps
Dinner: Cauliflower Crust Pizza topped with Tomato Sauce, Mozzarella, and Pepperoni
Snacks/Desserts: Bell Pepper Nachos, Oven-Baked Cinnamon Apple Chips

Appendix

Glossary of Terms

Metabolism - The sum of all chemical processes in the body that convert food into energy and maintain life. This includes fat burning, protein synthesis and other energy-requiring functions.

Metabolic Rate - The amount of energy expended in a given time frame, often measured in calories per day. Basal metabolic rate (BMR) describes energy used at rest.

Metabolic Flexibility - The ability to readily adapt fuel oxidation to fuel availability. Flexibility allows switching between burning fats or carbohydrates efficiently based on needs.

Metabolic Confusion - Strategically manipulating diet and exercise to continually challenge the body and avoid plateaus. Preventing adaptation spikes fat burning.

Macronutrients - The major nutritional components that provide calories: protein, carbohydrates and fat. Balancing macronutrients optimally fuels metabolism.

Micronutrients - Essential vitamins and minerals needed in small amounts that support enzymatic processes. Micronutrient adequacy is required for optimal metabolism.

Protein - Macronutrients composed of amino acids that serve as the body's structural building blocks and facilitate tissue repair. Protein is essential for preserving muscle mass.

Carbohydrates - Macronutrients that are the body's main initial fuel source. Carbs include sugars, starches, and fiber. They replenish glycogen stores.

Fats - Highly concentrated macronutrients that provide energy and support many bodily functions. Healthy fats should be included in moderation.

Calorie - A unit measuring the energy content of foods. A calorie surplus contributes to weight gain over time, while a deficit promotes fat loss.

Calorie Cycling - Strategically varying calorie intake day-to-day or week-to-week. Oscillating caloric amounts helps overcome plateaus.

Insulin - A hormone secreted by the pancreas that allows cells to utilize glucose from carbohydrates. It controls blood sugar levels.

Glucose - Simple sugar and key source of energy from carbohydrate digestion. It circulates in the blood to fuel cells.

Glycogen - The stored form of glucose in muscles and the liver that serves as an energy reserve source.

Ketosis - A metabolic state where the body switches to primarily burning fat rather than glucose for fuel through ketone production.

Gluconeogenesis - The metabolic process of producing new glucose molecules from sources like protein, lactate or glycerol.

Carb Cycling - Strategically varying carbohydrate intake to match activity levels day-to-day. This metabolic confusion technique maximizes fat burning.

Intermittent Fasting - An eating pattern that alternates between periods of fasting and eating. It allows metabolic resetting.

Nutrient Timing - Strategically scheduling meals and food choices around physical activity to optimize performance and recovery.

Nutrient Partitioning - Regulating nutrition so calories are optimally utilized for energy, muscle growth, and other metabolic needs.

Metabolic Damage - Disruption of normal metabolism often following extreme or prolonged calorie restriction.

Plateau - The inability to continue progressing despite adherence. Metabolic confusion overcomes plateaus.

Set Point - The weight range your body aims to maintain based on genetic and environmental factors. This can be gradually lowered.

Macronutrient Ratios - The recommended balance of macronutrients (proteins, carbs, fats) suited for different goals like weight loss or muscle gain.

These key terms represent the foundational language and concepts for implementing metabolic flexibility strategies successfully. Let this glossary guide you on the path towards lifelong health.

CREDITS

SCAN THE QR-CODE:

Made in the USA
Columbia, SC
18 February 2025

54023461R00057